the
Mental
edge

Maximize Your Sports Potential
with the Mind-Body Connection

KENNETH BAUM

with Richard Trubo

A Perigee Book

In memory of Mark Tornberg,
my first workout partner and best buddy . . .
I turned the loss into a gain

A Perigee Book
Published by The Berkley Publishing Group
A division of Penguin Putnam Inc.
375 Hudson Street
New York, New York 10014

First edition: March 1999

Published simultaneously in Canada.

The Penguin Putnam Inc. World Wide Web site address is
www.penguinputnam.com

Library of Congress Cataloging-in-Publication Data

Baum, Kenneth.
    The mental edge : maximize your sports potential with the
mind-body connection / Kenneth Baum with Richard Trubo. — 1st ed.
        p.   cm.
    "A Perigee book."
    ISBN 0-399-52481-9
    1. Sports—Psychological aspects.   2. Imagery (Psychology)
3. Visualization.   I. Trubo, Richard.   II. Title.
GV706.4.B38   1999
796'.01—dc21   98-49937
                                                            CIP

Printed in the United States of America

10   9   8   7   6   5   4

ATHLETES ACROSS AMERICA
PRAISE KENNETH BAUM AND HIS
NATIONALLY ACCLAIMED MENTAL EDGE
PERFORMANCE PROGRAM

"Ken's technique helped me to win my first international medal."
—Rodrigo Gonzales, 100 meter freestyle, three-time All American UCLA Bruins, Bronze Medalist Pan American Games

"I had one vault over nineteen feet in my life. After working with Ken I had five vaults over nineteen feet in one year!"
—Dean Starkey, Pole Vault, number one in the U.S. and number two in the world

"Incredible results! I'm playing better than ever and having a great time."
—Nick Panino, Soccer All American La Canada H.S., Scholarship UCLA Bruins, National Champion Club: High School, College

"Going to college from high school, I was unsure. Ken's training helped my confidence, my skill improved and I played at a higher level."
—Pam Gradoville, Basketball, All-Time Leading Scorer, Creighton University

"I've matured as a player and my mom says as a person. I'm definitely a better player since working with Ken."
—Daniel Wilson, Softball, Esperanza H.S., Scholarship University of Florida

Contents

Foreword

by Karch Kiraly

As Ken Baum mentions in *The Mental Edge,* I'm always looking for ways to train and improve. That may sound strange for someone who has won three Olympic gold medals. But I believe there's still plenty of room for improvement in my game. Why do I try to get better? Because I might attempt to compete in my fourth Olympics in the year 2000. Even though I'm thirty-seven years old, I want to push the envelope and see how good I can become and for how long. I want to keep an edge on the competition, even though the competition keeps getting stronger. I've also never seen any team play the perfect game of volleyball—that is, winning a game 15-0 on fifteen straight serves (although we still strive for it!).

For all these reasons, I subscribe to Ken's Performance Stretcher #2: "If you do what you've always done, you'll get what you've always gotten." And so I change. Some of the weapons I've added to the arsenal in the last few years include a new stretching and movement program, a different strength program, and relaxation training to manage the stress of Olympic competition. One part of my game that I had neglected was mental toughness. I didn't learn mental toughness through any organized program, though I wish I had; I learned it instead by experience—playing beach volleyball as a kid against grown men.

You have to be mentally tough to be a world-class volleyball player, but I find beach volleyball uniquely demanding. You might have to play seven hours in 100-degree temperatures and 90 percent humidity during the course of a July or August event. With only two players on each team, there are no substitutions and there's nowhere to hide if your game has weaknesses that can be exploited. It's no wonder that only seven players in history have amassed sixty or more career victories; they are the seven best known for their willpower and strength under duress. The athletes who have the Mental Edge win tournaments; the athletes who don't, don't. It's that simple.

If you are looking for a way to improve your game, try *The Mental Edge*. With Ken's book, you now have the opportunity to learn that kind of mental toughness in a systematic, organized way. I have found his ideas to have remarkable common sense; I also discovered that I had been using some of his techniques without even realizing it.

I wish you the best of luck. Enjoy.

Acknowledgments

The Mental Edge materialized after years of research that began with a spark ignited by John Wooden, the legendary basketball coach. He proved that mental training does work. I appreciate his pioneering work and applications.

Thanks to Dave Meyers and Swen Nater, former players for Coach Wooden. They provided me with insights that came from being at the receiving end of Wooden's early techniques.

Special thanks to the editorial team:

- Richard Trubo, who saw this book before I did;

- Jane Dystel for taking a chance on me;

- Sheila Curry for her editing expertise and patience;

- Karch Kiraly for being a living testimony to the Mental Edge, and proving that nice guys can finish first.

Special acknowledgment to Merja Connolly and Charlie Schober of UCI Athletics, who keep trying to find a way; Dr. Howard Fox for being one of the good guys; and all the coaches around the world—like Rich Wordes and

Frank Godino—who do it "for the kids." May you be blessed.

Finally, what would an acknowledgments page of my first book be without thanking my wonderful parents, who let me follow my dreams.

—Kenneth Baum

Finding the
Mental Edge

A forty-one-year-old man plays golf twice a week, but his putting has stubbornly remained the worst part of his game. "I've gradually changed everything else for the better," he says. "But when it comes to putting, I've hit a wall. I don't know how I'm going to get past that barrier."

A twenty-three-year-old professional tennis player has become anxious about his inconsistent backhand. "The other parts of my game are just fine," he says. "But it's gotten to the point where I'm thinking too much about my backhand. Whenever a ball is hit to my backhand side, I don't have the confidence that I'm going to be able to return it with any authority—or return it at all."

A thirty-one-year-old woman who began jogging two years ago wants to improve her times in the 10-kilometer "fun runs" in which she participates. "I compete against myself," she says, "and try to knock a few seconds off my time in each race. But I've been stuck lately and haven't been able to improve my times."

These three people are having experiences similar to those of many thousands of others, from professional athletes who play their sport for money to "weekend jocks" who participate in sports solely for the fun of it. Whether they're playing in the National Football League or for a community softball team, they're looking to get better at their game. They are seeking an edge that will allow them to putt with more accuracy, pitch the baseball with more speed, or get a few more strikes during a Friday night at the bowling alley.

This book is written for people like them—and like you. It will help you understand what separates the average athlete from the good or the great ones. It will explain how athletes at all levels can use not only their bodies, but also their minds, and merge them in perfect harmony to achieve their full potential. Most important, it will teach you, step by step, how to use these same mind-body strategies. In short, it will give you the Mental Edge.

Over the years, you might have wondered how two athletes with virtually identical body types and physical capabilities could run at such dramatically different speeds, or throw the football with such varying accuracy. Why does one become an elite athlete, consistently outperforming his competitors, while the other is always overshadowed by his rivals? Why do athletes with seemingly average physical attributes excel at their sport, whereas those with much greater potential never reach their dreams? While it's true that an individual's physical training and workouts are crucial factors, the extra edge or advantage is just as likely to come from the mental game.

This is an exciting time in both amateur and professional sports. You can take advantage of the new science of mentally driven athletic achievement that is allowing people to run faster, jump higher, and hit the ball with greater bat speed than ever before. It will help you unleash your own potential in whatever sport you participate, no matter what your level of play. It can help you tap into your mind's tremendous power, getting more out of your workouts and performing better during competition. If you experience fear or anxiety while competing, you'll learn how to control and conquer it. If you lack confidence on the field, you'll find ways to develop it. In the process, you'll grow into the best athlete you can possibly become. That's a promise. I can make that promise because I have successfully taught these techniques to a wide range of athletes and seen great results.

The Mental Edge is a concrete program that will significantly improve your game. It involves specific, proven techniques—setting goals, strengthening your belief in yourself, improving your concentration, using imagery, overcoming obstacles, and conquering anxiety, among others. Every exercise is strongly based in science. Each one contributes to the power of the rest. And if you incorporate all of them into your own athletic life, your performance *will* improve. I've seen it happen to athletes at all levels. With this step-by-step program, it *will* happen for you, too.

Are You Maximizing Your Potential?

When I first started working with Dean Starkey, he was already an elite pole vaulter. Even so, he could not win consistently in major track meets. In fact, Dean had cleared the 19-foot level only once in competition, although he felt he should be soaring above that height meet after meet. He had worked with sports psychologists in the past, but he never seemed to be able to translate what he had learned to the track. He was at an impasse, unable to clear 19 feet again and mired in a quicksand of growing frustration. At the same time, with a major track-and-field meet on the horizon, he was becoming more anxious over his poor vaulting during practices. "Why can't I get over nineteen feet again?" he asked. "Why is this happening?"

Dean and I scheduled a series of sessions together during a two-month period. I introduced him to many of the techniques you will read about in this book—goal setting, visualization, and Power Talk, among others. Most significantly, I helped him work on a powerful process—the Success History Search—one that he had never been exposed to before. By using this technique, he tapped into the full experience of his best previous vault. While in a state of relaxation, he was able to see and feel the most subtle nuances of a 19-foot vault—not just the physical mechanics of the vault itself, but everything from the expression on his face and the sound of his breathing to the smells surrounding the track and the noises of the crowd. These feelings became so vivid in his mind's eye that it was as though the vault were really happening all over again.

Then Dean began to integrate this experience into the present moment. He created a "performance ritual" that he began to use in both practices and competition. We would work at the track on the mental preparation he would do before he would pick up the pole. His confidence—and his vaulting—began to improve.

As this is being written, Dean is vaulting better than ever. He now frequently clears the bar at 19 feet. He took second place in the 1997 World Championships and is a leading candidate for a medal in the 2000 Summer Olympic Games. As Dean said, "I went from having one vault over nineteen feet in my life, and then after working with the Mental Edge, having five vaults over nineteen feet in one year!" He has been shattering that barrier consistently ever since.

In the competitive world of sports, many athletes—whether amateur or professional—are looking for an edge. Some remain convinced that the only way to improve their performance is to lengthen their workouts by an extra thirty or sixty minutes a day. Or change their diet in some way. Or even turn to anabolic steroids or another type of illegal (and possibly life-threatening) drug.

But, in fact, the most potent performance enhancer you have is the three pounds of gray matter located between your ears. It is more powerful than any other mechanism that you'll find. And by using it in the ways I'll describe in this book, *you can improve your performance by up to 40 percent*. That's right—*40 percent*. This is a startling but proven fact.

For fourteen years I've been working with athletes of all calibers . . . the once-a-week tennis player trying to improve her serve . . . the professional baseball player attempting to master the subtleties of hitting a ball to the opposite field . . . the world-class track stars at the Elite Training Institute, a satellite training center for the U.S. Olympic team in Santa Monica, California. I've taught the Mental Edge to high school volleyball teams, college basketball stars, and National Football League wide receivers. But no matter what their level, if they have taken this program seriously, they have improved. Without fail.

Letting Your Body Take Over

This is not a program about behavioral psychology. Yes, you'll learn something about how the mind and the body can work together, and the physiology behind it. But more than anything, we'll concentrate on how you can become a better athlete. Even if you're skeptical as we get started, I believe that your attitude will change as your performance improves. Again, this program works for everyone, regardless of age, sex, or skill level. By using the Mental Edge, you can play any sport better.

Ironically, even though this book is called *The Mental Edge,* a lot of what you'll learn will involve using your mind in ways that will allow your *body* to do exactly what it already knows how to do. Too often athletes are crippled by what I call "analysis paralysis." Whether they're a basketball player standing at the free-throw line preparing to throw a foul shot or a soccer player getting ready for a penalty kick on goal, they make the mistake of overanalyzing what they're about to do. Thus, by the time the actual moment to perform has arrived, they're almost doomed to fail. Instead of mentally "standing back" and letting their body work the way it has been trained to, they get in its way and sabotage its best efforts.

For example, if you're a golfer, when you approach the tee, do you find yourself saying, "Okay, keep your head down . . . let your left arm guide your backswing . . . keep your right arm straight . . . "? By instructing yourself through every tiny detail, your body may become overwhelmed by trying to do everything just right—and the ball will probably end up in the rough rather than on the green, spoiling an otherwise perfect Saturday morning!

Remember, your body knows exactly what to do. That's what it has learned during all of those golf lessons and all of those hours on the driving range. When you're finally on the course, you need to move away from the analytical left side of your brain and let the more creative, visual right side take over. Let your body do its thing, while you analyze less. By the time you're in the midst of competition, you need to let things happen. And that's what you'll learn to do in this book.

Over the years, I've discovered that every change in your mental or emotional state is accompanied by a corresponding shift in your physical state. So a key part of the Mental Edge is learning to minimize your mind's distracting and counterproductive messages and signals to your body. Essentially you'll be conditioning your body to perform instinctively and unconsciously, guided by the feelings of success and confidence that you've already built into your mind and body, and automatically triggering the connections that make it possible for you to achieve at the highest possible level of performance. You'll create a state of mind-body integration conducive to both a physical and a mental edge that will allow your mind to step back and let your body do what it has been prepared to do. You'll learn to pay attention, and then let go.

Here's a simple example of what I'm talking about. A few years ago I was bowling with friends. Winning didn't matter; I was interested only in having fun. To my surprise, however, I bowled very well in the first game. Everything my body had learned about bowling in previous years was still in place. Time after time, the ball headed directly into the 1-3 pocket, usually sending all of the pins flying. I was on a roll.

But rather than enjoying the experience, I immediately started to analyze what I was doing. I began thinking, "If my release were just a little better, I think I could have converted every one of those opportunities for spares!"

So I picked apart my form . . . the height of my backswing, the position of my feet, my follow-through after the delivery. And guess what happened? My game (and my ego!) fell apart. The second game was just terrible, with the ball bouncing erratically down the alley. Rather than wondering if I was going to get a strike or a spare, I was wondering if the ball would land in the gutter!

While awaiting the third game I could have panicked and begun analyzing even more. But I caught myself, and returned to the principles of the Mental Edge. I set aside all of the analysis and just let my body do what it had been doing successfully in the first game—and I bowled just fine.

In fact, once you've prepared yourself, letting your body take over is key—with just a bit of additional mental preparation before you pick up the bowling ball, the tennis racket, or the putter. Through training, your body already has learned how to perform at its peak. So at the moment you're approaching the high-jump bar or running a pass pattern toward the end zone, the Mental Edge will allow you to step back and let your body do what it knows how to do.

At the world-class level in particular, the differences in physical capabilities among athletes are negligible. The real difference is the Mental Edge. If you're an elite athlete, the difference between winning a medal and finishing in the middle of the pack is often your ability to prepare yourself mentally to get the best results from your body, free of self-doubts and overanalysis. When the starting gun fires, the Mental Edge will allow you to place complete trust in your body.

My Own Learning Curve

I've played sports for as long as I can remember. Baseball. Basketball. Football. If there was a ball involved, I was eager to bounce it, hit it, kick it, or throw it. The phrase "couch potato" was not part of my vocabulary. Although basketball was my primary sport in high school and college, I also ran track, primarily the 440. In my mid-twenties I began competing in triathlons, too. I still play beach volleyball (it's an almost inevitable part of living in the sun-bathed coastal cities of Southern California).

When basketball was my obsession, however, I knew nothing about the mental side of sports. As a result, my performance suffered at times. One incident sticks in my mind as a classic example of how easy it is to become mentally distracted, at the expense of playing well. To put the story in context, I lived to play basketball. It was my number-one love (girls were a close second). But as my senior year in high school began, an article appeared in the local newspaper quoting my basketball coach's evaluation of our team's outlook. He couldn't have been more complimentary when he described me as the team's best athlete, best defensive player, and the "toughest kid on the court." However, he added, "Ken doesn't have much of a shot."

Not much of a shot! Instantly those words shook my self-confidence and left it in ruins. Throughout that basketball season I kept thinking, "He's such a great coach;

he's such a great judge of talent. If he says I'm a lousy shooter, I must be a lousy shooter." And so I proved him right. Free throws that I had made easily the previous season bounced harmlessly off the rim. Jump shots sometimes didn't even hit the rim. With each missed shot my confidence waned further, and I was terrified that the coach would get angry. I became ever more preoccupied with that quote in the newspaper, and one terrible game followed another. When college scouts were in the stands watching me, I played even worse. I didn't have the mental skills to deal effectively with what was happening to me, and my coach's preseason observation became a self-fulfilling prophecy. I continued to try to please my coach by not making mistakes, but I realized that the best way to avoid mistakes was to stop shooting altogether. My dream of playing college basketball was slipping away. In the process, basketball stopped being fun.

Amid this personal turmoil a much greater tragedy occurred: my best friend committed suicide. I was devastated. Like me, he hadn't achieved the goals he had set for himself in sports, and he was crushed with disappointment. His death overwhelmed me. In the middle of the school term I quit playing sports altogether.

In the months and years that followed I began reading about and studying human psychology, trying to better understand what had happened to my friend, and secondarily, how the mind could be used to ensure that sports participation would be a source of enjoyment and success, not one of stress and anxiety. When I wasn't reading, I attended classes and enrolled in seminars. I familiarized myself with the evidence gathered through new technologies such as CAT (computerized axial tomography) and PET (positron emission tomography) scans, which pinpoint the brain pathways used in sports-related mental processes such as visualization.

Early in my studies I recognized that all behavior, including the behavior of our bodies, can ultimately be traced back to the brain. Words and particularly images in the brain can influence physical activity, including the way we perform on the basketball court, the soccer field, or the racquetball court. The connection of brain and body formed the foundation on which the Mental Edge was built. Over the years, my own principles and strategies for maximizing sports performance gradually evolved, and I tried them out first on myself and then on others.

As I began to work with athletes I immediately saw the potential benefits of involving the mind in sports. Not too many years ago, if a field-goal kicker wanted to refine his skills, he had only one avenue to pursue: he would work with a kicking coach, fine-tuning his mechanics. He might stay late after practice and kick an extra twenty-five footballs toward the uprights. And, in fact, he might become a better kicker in the process. But as valuable as that approach may be, the Mental Edge could have given him an additional weapon that might have made the difference between sending the ball sailing perfectly through the goal posts or having it veer off to the left or right in the final seconds of a pressure-packed, regular season game. It could have helped him stay completely focused on the task at hand, ignoring the distractions and the pressures of competition.

Perhaps you recall the inspiring story of speed skater Dan Jansen. Competing in the 1988 Winter Olympics on the day his sister died, Jansen fell while skating at a record-shattering pace in the 500-meter race; it was a race he was expected to win before stress sabotaged a lifetime of physical training.

The mind, Jansen learned, can be the athlete's greatest ally—or a powerful enemy. So Jansen worked on the mental side of his sport, and soon returned to competition. In the 1994 Winter Games he raced not only in the 500-meter event, but also in the 1000-meter race . . . an event he had hated for years. He admitted worrying about how he would perform at that longer distance; he feared running out of energy in the last half of the race. That attitude could have set him up for failure were he not working on the mental side of his sport. For two years his mental training became as important as his physical workouts. So not surprisingly, equipped with the tools to succeed, he captured a gold in the 1,000 meters.

The Mental Edge's Track Record

Athletes like Dan Jansen aren't alone in recognizing that there's more to success on the rink, the court, or the field than just having the physical ability to play the game well. Many coaches and even team owners now acknowledge it, too. In recent years I've served as a consultant for coaches in the National Hockey League and for Seattle Supersonics coach George Karl. I've counseled the staff of the Kansas City Royals. I've taught my program to Brooks Johnson, the U.S. Olympic sprinting coach (he helped Carl Lewis run to medal-winning performances). I've also worked with many athletes themselves, such as Mike Reddick, the Oakland Raiders and Canadian Football League pass receiver who overcame the obstacle of his diminutive size in a sport of giants and conquered the psychological barriers that were causing passes to slip through his fingertips. The Mental Edge has also helped swimmers, like Rodrigo Gonzales, who shattered his own insecurities to win a bronze medal at the Pan American Games.

Pam Gradoville was one of the first athletes with whom I worked. She was a talented high school basketball player with all of the physical attributes to play at the college level, but she wasn't confident that she could do it. On the court she often played timidly, as though she were just waiting for an opponent to run through her or shoot over her. She constantly compared herself to other talented players, and often felt inferior to them. There was more press attention paid to them, and she assumed they must be better than she. In short, she didn't believe in herself.

I began meeting with Pam, and we worked on changing her thinking and boosting her self-confidence. She began to see herself as a talented player, whether or not she was getting attention from the press or from college recruiters. We worked on stepping up her aggressiveness on the court. At 5'11", she was definitely going to find herself playing the post in college. But she needed to become a tougher player in the inside game.

I had Pam sit down with a sheet of paper and write down all of her strengths and weaknesses. First she focused on her strengths, and she began to visualize them by experiencing them fully in her mind's eye. As she focused on the things she did well, her self-confidence grew. Next she turned to her weaknesses. But rather than letting them sabotage her, she approached them with a positive mindset, determined to transform them into strengths. Over the weeks, she worked on overcoming those weaknesses one at a time so her task didn't seem overwhelming. She made up her mind to play more aggressively. She began to perceive herself as tougher and more tenacious under the hoop—and she soon translated that into a more intense performance on the court. She made very quick progress, and college scouts recognized it.

"The mental training helped my confidence enormously," she said. "That allowed my skills to improve, and I began playing at a higher level." Much higher. Pam won a full scholarship to Creighton University and became an outstanding basketball player there. In fact, she ultimately became Creighton's all-time leading scorer!

What's the Evidence?

As the Mental Edge program has evolved, I've always insisted that it be grounded in science. No hunches. No wild theories. Not only have I based it on my ongoing research with both weekend athletes and world-class performers, but I've also used the latest studies at institutions like Harvard and Stanford as its foundation. In the next chapter I'll explain further the remarkable research into the mental side of sports. For now let me mention a persuasive study conducted in the Soviet Union that caught my interest early in my development of the Mental Edge and helped convince me of the value of mental training. In the study, which began as the Soviets were preparing for the 1980 Winter Olympic Games, their elite athletes were assigned to one of four training programs. The first group consisted of athletes who spent all of their time on physical training. A second group devoted 75 percent of its time to physical training and 25 percent to mental training. A third group divided its time equally between physical and mental regimens; and the final group spent 25 percent on the physical aspects of training and 75 percent on the mental side.

The results of the study were astounding. The more time that athletes devoted to mental training, the more they improved! Those who made the greatest strides spent the majority of their time (75 percent) on the mental aspects of sports. The least progress was achieved by the athletes who worked exclusively on physical training. These findings were precisely the opposite of what many experts expected, particularly those who are disciples of the "no pain, no gain" philosophy.

The bottom line of the Soviet study: the mental side of sports can unlock your physical potential. By devoting time to mental training, you will be able to spend less time in your physical training—and when you do work out on the practice field, you'll be training smarter and more efficiently. In essence, you'll be getting more out of less.

Bringing Enjoyment Back into Sports

The psychological problems I described earlier relative to my own high school sports experience aren't unique. So often athletes tell me, "Playing my sport just isn't fun anymore." The reason is simple: the pressure they feel to excel drains the pleasure from their game. In my case, I had a great time playing "pick-up" games (and still do), where I was competing for the sheer joy of it. But in front of a crowd in a basketball arena, I just didn't have the skills that could have helped me find pleasure in competition—*and* perform better.

Fortunately the Mental Edge can help you do that. For example, it has assisted swimmer David McGlyn, who competed for the University of California at Irvine. The pressure to win was getting to him, and as hard as he tried, he couldn't improve his times. He felt defeated, and told me, "All the fun is gone." As a result, he considered giving up the sport.

David and I began working together. In the beginning, I reminded him that he was competing in a sport in which men peak in their twenties, and that at age eighteen, he should still be improving, and enjoying his successes. So as a starting point, he needed to answer the questions, "Do *I* really want to swim? Do I want to swim for *myself*, and not because I don't want to disappoint my parents and my coach?" He gave it some thought and finally said, "Sure, I do want to swim. I'd like to recapture the fun I used to have swimming. I'd like to start improving again. And I don't want to be a quitter. I'm afraid that if I quit now, I'll be a quitter throughout my entire life."

With that as a springboard we began focusing on how David could make swimming enjoyable again. "We're going to stop worrying about winning and about your times," I told him. "We're going to concentrate on the process of swimming." Out of the water David began using the Success History Search (which you'll learn about in chapter 6), and as he did, he began to feel the joy he had once experienced through swimming, and the natural flow of his body as it moved in the water. In his mind he relived the sensations of pushing off from the starting platform, gliding into the pool, and propelling himself through the water. Those images and feelings became his driving force, the sensations that he wanted to recapture in competition. And he became excited about the prospect of turning swimming into a positive experience again.

Then we added a technique in which he selected a keyword that, when repeated at poolside, would instantly put him into a frame of mind to perform to his full potential, and with joy. Almost immediately he began swimming for the fun of it, and when that happened, he started swimming faster, too. In fact, he began winning races. As a junior, he recorded his fastest times ever. I also started working with his teammates on the mental side of swimming, and they exceeded all expectations by finishing second in the Big West Conference.

Taking the First Step

Ironically, although many athletes have heard about the mental side of sports, some continue to reject sports psychology outright, proclaiming, "No one's going to mess with my head." So instead they'll spend $50 on a can of protein powder. They'll buy a new tennis racket for $300. They'll purchase a new pair of running shoes for $150. Each of these additions might help in its own way. But nothing will improve their athletic performance as consistently and for as long a time as mental training. Months and years after their shoes have worn out, their tennis racket has broken, and their protein powder container is empty, the Mental Edge can still be a positive force in their lives.

Nevertheless, as you prepare to get started in this program, keep in mind that it will provide you with skills, not miracles. It may give you instantaneous success, but it may be that your improvements are more gradual and constant instead. Best of all, the tools are accessible to everyone. So often, athletes who work with sports psychologists find it hard work, and difficult to apply what they've learned to their day-to-day workouts and in competition. But this program, they tell me, is very user-friendly. It works for young and old, and at every level of athletic prowess.

Occasionally a weekend athlete will say, "Look, I play tennis three or four times a month; I don't want to be spending all of my free time doing this mental stuff." Frankly, this program is particularly useful for these part-time athletes. After all, they don't have time to spend five, ten, or twenty hours a week practicing on the tennis court to perfect their game. But if they devote just *fifteen to twenty minutes* during the week to working on mental training skills and *ten minutes* before the start of competition applying these techniques, they *will* play better. If you're hoping to cut a few strokes off your weekend golf scores, swim faster in an organized masters' program, or run a marathon, the techniques in this book will allow you reach your goals and fuel your love of the game.

Again, it won't require a huge time commitment. My clients have found that it initially takes only about six hours to learn the tools and already see improvements when using them. Then, to make the results even more powerful, they spend about fifteen to twenty minutes a week away from the field or court refining them. That's all. The minutes they devote to mental training are very limited, compared to the hours that typical athletes spend on the training field (although most coaches will still tell you that the only way to improve is to practice, practice, practice). In fact, as the study in the Soviet Union showed, to get the most out of your athletic performance, it may be advantageous to spend less time on the field and more time on mental training.

If you make a commitment to the Mental Edge your performance *will* improve, and you'll have more fun as it happens—no matter what your present level. Not long ago I worked with my own fifteen-year-old daughter, who is a fine young athlete but certainly not at a world-class level (not yet, at least!). One of her sports is track-and-field, and I taught her two visualization techniques, which she began putting into action immediately. What effect did they have on her performance? After just this single visualization session, she cut three-tenths of a second off her time in the 100-yard dash and added a foot on to her long jump! After one session!

Of course every person is different, physically and mentally. But as you're about to find out, *everyone* can play better using the Mental Edge.

Merging Science
and Sports

How many good athletes do you know who have stopped short of realizing their potential? They were the baseball players who should have consistently hit .300, but never exceeded .275 . . . the sprinters who had the promise of breaking the 10-second barrier in the 100-meter dash, but seemed stuck at 10.3 . . . the basketball guards whose free-throw percentage never exceeded 70 percent in game situations, even though they shot much better during practices.

Perhaps you knew someone like this in high school or college? Or maybe you yourself fit this description: you've had more room to grow athletically, but just haven't been able to break through. Too often, after years of disappointment, athletes in this situation simply give up. As their frustration level climbs it overwhelms their commitment to excel and they begin to accept their fate of being a "second-tier" player. In some cases they don't even try out for the school team; it's simply easier to give up before they start rather than risk the embarrassment of being cut from the team.

For every athlete who quits before reaching his dream another has found a way to go for the gold. If you ever saw Larry Bird shoot jump shots for the Boston Celtics, you might find it hard to believe that he was only an above-average high school player. No one ever foresaw him making it to the NBA, much less becoming one of the greatest players in basketball history. But Bird made it happen. So did Brett Butler, who was told repeatedly that he was too small to play major-league baseball. Everyone seemed to believe it—except Butler. His never-say-quit attitude drove him to work overtime . . . building his strength, improving his speed, and refining his attitude. When Butler retired in 1997, he could look back at a successful and rewarding baseball career with the Atlanta Braves, San Francisco Giants, Los Angeles Dodgers, and New York Mets.

If you're an athlete with untapped potential, the Mental Edge can help you climb aboard the fast track to developing your potential. In my own work with athletes at every level, I've seen the mental side of sports give men and women an added advantage that has elevated them from the junior varsity to the varsity, or has lifted them from a benchwarmer into the starting lineup.

At the world-class level, every athlete is looking for even the smallest edge. In the track sprints at the 1992 Olympic Games, for example, the time difference between the gold and silver medal winners averaged about two-tenths of a second! Even a small improvement in performance is crucial, and that's where the Mental Edge has been able to help. When athletes approach this program with the same seriousness they do their physical training, it can help them run faster, jump higher, and throw harder than they ever have before.

Without the Mental Edge, swimmer Rodrigo Gonzales might never have stepped onto the victory stand at the Pan American Games in Cuba with a medal around his neck.

He was an all-American swimmer at UCLA, but his performance had plateaued in his junior year. Although he had already competed in the Olympics, he had not lived up to his own expectations. He had never finished better than fifteenth in international competition. With the Pan Am Games on the horizon, he was in a psychological funk, feeling frustrated and discouraged. He had convinced himself that at age twenty-one he was simply too old to improve his time in the 100-meter freestyle. "Just look at history," he told me, with an "I give up" sigh in his voice. "Swimmers peak at a much younger age than I am."

Amid those Methuselah-like feelings of being past his prime, a part of Rodrigo still felt that he could get better and faster, if he could just figure out how. That's when he began working with me and my program. Frankly, our first two sessions together didn't go very well; the techniques were very different from anything he had been exposed to, and he became skeptical about whether it could really help. For years he had been told by swimming coaches that "guts" is all he really needed to succeed; one coach had said, "If you've got guts, you'll become a great swimmer; if you don't, you might as well never bother getting onto the starting platform." Well, Rodrigo had guts, but he still wasn't performing at the level he wanted to achieve.

Gradually, however, Rodrigo started to recognize the value of the Mental Edge. His negative attitude, he acknowledged, had become like a 500-pound anchor tied around his waist. He also couldn't deny that "older" athletes like Nolan Ryan and Carl Lewis continued to perform at peak levels far beyond their so-called prime. I also showed him statistics demonstrating that many speed athletes—whether on the running track or in the pool—actually hit their peak in their twenties. For Rodrigo, that was an eye-opener that dramatically changed his outlook.

With the passage of time Rodrigo began to define his *true* potential. He trained aggressively using both physical and mental techniques. He started to visualize what it would feel like to swim faster, and in his mind's eye he could see himself skimming through the water with the grace of a dolphin and the aggressiveness of a shark. By the end of our sessions together he had become such a skilled visualizer that while he sat in a chair and used the imagery he had learned, I could see major muscle firings and changes in his breathing patterns. He could feel his respiration becoming more labored as he pictured himself closing in on the finish line. And as he played out the race in his mind, he could actually time his visualization within a fraction of a second of his desired real-time swim. He had learned to make the proper neurological connections—and before long, it began to pay off in the pool. He started to outswim competitors who were years younger than he. As his confidence climbed, he knocked precious ticks off his time, and his expectations soared. Whereas he once thought that he'd be lucky to finish eighth place in the Pan American Games, he began to see himself as a medalist.

In Cuba, when Rodrigo reached the finish line at the Pan Am Games, he had swum his fastest time ever. In the process, he had won the bronze, his first international medal.

What the Research Shows

As I mentioned in chapter 1, when I introduce the Mental Edge to athletes I occasionally encounter skepticism and raised eyebrows. A few have said something like, "This New Age stuff just isn't for me! I'm just fine working out in the weight room!" But once they're aware of the impressive body of research into the mind-body connection, their hesitancy comes to a screeching halt that burns the rubber on the soles of their workout shoes. Athletes and coaches can't deny that mental training really does work.

Of course there is really nothing new about sports psychology in general. More than 2,000 years ago Greek runners were not permitted to compete if they became pale just before their event, since this was deemed to be a sign of fear. The Greeks also believed that soothing music could calm an excitable athlete just prior to his race, and thus allow him to perform better.

Now, of course, there is science to support the hunches that drove some of the earliest efforts at sports psychology. Here are just a few of the studies that have convinced me that when it comes to athletic achievement, mental training is as important as pumping iron.

• At Hunter College, seventy-two players from eight college basketball teams participated in a study in which they worked on the mental side of shooting free throws. One group began each day's basketball practice with a relaxation technique, followed by visualization or mental rehearsal in which they imagined every detail of their foul shooting: they pictured preparing for the shot at the free-throw line, bouncing the ball a few times, raising their shooting arm with the ball balanced in their palm, bending at the knees, and releasing the ball toward the basket. Using this technique, the shooting accuracy of these athletes improved by 7 percent—a change so significant that coaches reported that the better shooting produced eight additional wins during the season.

As part of the Hunter College study these athletes were hooked up to sensors that measured their neuromuscular activity during mental training. It showed that the same muscles used in free-throw shooting were activated during the practice of imagery. Thus, on a subtle level, the body itself was actually going through the motions of free-throw shooting.

· A 1991 study found that there was no age barrier to visualization. The research involved 120 seventh-grade students who played field hockey, some of whom combined relaxation plus imagery with their physical practice. The students in the relaxation/imagery group improved their accuracy in hitting field-hockey targets by a startling 160 percent! Those who participated only in physical practice improved, too, but by less than half as much (a 70 percent improvement).

· Researchers at the Olympic Training Center in Colorado enlisted thirty college-age golfers, who were asked to work on their putting each day for a week. One group was instructed to visualize sinking each putt just before tapping the ball toward the hole. They were told to picture the entire process—from the backswing before the ball is struck to the ball rolling into the center of the cup. A second group was instructed to do the same, but with one change: in their imagination, they were asked to picture the ball veering to the left or the right just as it approached the hole, stopping just inches from the cup. A third group only practiced putting, without doing any visualization.

When the week was over, the students in the first group had improved their putting accuracy by 30 percent; by comparison, the group who did no visualizing but physically practiced their putting showed improvements as well, by 11 percent. Most intriguing, the middle group—those who had pictured the golf ball straying off course, away from the cup—experienced a worsening of their putting; their accuracy declined by 21 percent over the course of the week. They had pictured themselves putting poorly—and they did.

Results from other studies have been just as persuasive. At Harvard University, researchers implemented a sports mental training program incorporating meditation techniques. After five weeks participants had cut 14.41 milliseconds off their response time to game-related stimuli. That's enough time to allow you to get to a tennis serve that you'd ordinarily miss. At Stanford University, imagery research has clearly demonstrated that three-dimensional visualized pictures can create dramatic and measurable physiological responses—from micromuscular activity to changes in breathing—identical to those that occur when athletes actually perform their sport.

Mind and Muscles

These studies are certainly impressive. But how does the mind influence the body so powerfully? While sitting in a chair in a state of relaxation, how can the mind activate physiological responses?

It is really not that much of a mystery. Here's the key: your central nervous system does not differentiate between real and imagined events. When you picture yourself swimming the 100-meter relay or kicking a 45-yard field goal through the uprights, the central nervous system responds as though it were really happening. In essence, sharp mental images, in which all of the senses are involved, are capable of "priming" and "pretraining" the body for a particular physical movement. This creates a pathway or connection between mind and body that promotes smoother and more precise physical activity once you actually get to the playing field. Thus, when you make the transition from an imagined to a real athletic performance your body has already been through a dress rehearsal and has a blueprint of every movement it should make. Your body knows what to expect and how it is supposed to function because it has already done so in response to your imagery. Mind and body have become fused, and they work together in an efficient, productive manner.

As I've already suggested, visualization can produce subtle muscle contractions that mirror the precise movements of the sports activity being imagined. For example, in a study in the *Journal of Sports Psychology*, weight lifters were asked to visualize themselves lifting a 25-pound dumbbell. During this process electromyographic

(EMG) measurements of their biceps were taken, which provided a record of the electrical activity associated with muscle movements. The result: during visualization, these men experienced significant biceps activity when compared to baseline recordings.

Formal studies aside, many of the world's top athletes have experienced transformations in their game using these techniques. Arnold Schwarzenegger was a pioneer in using his mind to help sculpt his body. In the 1960s and early 1970s he became an early proponent of visualization, picturing his biceps as mountains and imagining his calves just the way he wanted them to be. His workouts were consistently preceded by visualization sessions in which he would use his mind as an ally in shaping his body.

Skier Jean-Claude Killy had an injury that prevented him from practicing prior to a big race; as a result, his sole preparation for the race was through visualization. He repeatedly skied the course in his mind—and when the time came to actually navigate down the slopes, he skied what he described as one of the best races of his life.

Jack Nicklaus has told the story of the elaborate visualization process he has used for decades. Every aspect of his game is rehearsed in his mind before he ever approaches the first tee—from the swing of his club to the trajectory of the ball in flight to its bounce and roll on the green. According to Nicklaus, 40 percent of his game is setting up and assuming the proper stance, 10 percent is his swing, and the remaining 50 percent is the psychological game. He calls that mental side of the sport "going to the movies."

The Power of Self-Talk: The Evidence

The concept of self-talk is one I'll be discussing frequently in this book. All of us talk to ourselves throughout the day, both on and off the athletic field. If you come to the plate in the ninth inning of a crucial baseball game and you're thinking to yourself, "Just don't strike out like you did last time!" your chances of swinging futilely for a third strike are almost guaranteed. In reaction to negative self-talk, as you anxiously stand at the plate, you might unconsciously change your stance, or your muscles may react differently to the pitched ball. These subtle adjustments could sabotage your athletic performance.

If your self-talk is negative, it can leave you feeling anxious and afraid. Of course depending on the precise messages being communicated to your subconscious, self-talk can also dramatically *improve* your sports performance. Research shows that positive self-talk can make you more confident and focused.

At Springfield College, sports psychologist and tennis coach Judy Van Raalte, Ph.D., studied junior tennis players at U.S. Tennis Association tournaments. Some of these players frequently spoke aloud to themselves in a negative way during competition, saying things such as, "Why can't I serve?" and "Oh no, that was horrible!" Not surprisingly, Dr. Van Raalte found that these individuals were more likely to perform poorly during their matches.

Fortunately, as I'll explain in detail later, self-talk can be changed. If you're drowning in negative self-talk you can turn it around and use self-talk to your advantage. Consider a study in *The Behavior Therapist* in which researchers described working with a tennis player who was prone to talking to himself during matches, making statements such as, "You blew it!" and "Damn dummy!" The researchers instructed him on how to transform his self-talk into positive statements: "Stay cool," and "Okay, you double-faulted this time, but let's concentrate on the next serve!" After just one week of working with this new approach the player's winning percentage in deuce games during competition rose from 29 percent to 60 percent. He also said that the "feelings of disaster" that he often experienced just before matches had dissipated.

In your own life, has negative self-talk become a disruptive force? Has it interfered with your ability to remain focused and maintain good concentration? If so, your athletic performance has undoubtedly suffered. Imagine the baseball pitcher who begins talking to himself about the unnerving crowd noise at a key moment in the game . . . or the quarterback who becomes flustered as he stands over the center and begins self-talk about the unfamiliar defensive alignment on the other side of the line . . . or the basketball player, competing with a sprained ankle, who is preoccupied with his own self-talk about the pain he feels while fighting for a rebound. All of these athletes may perform poorly, inattentive to the task at hand.

The great athletes have refined their ability to stay focused despite the potential distractions around them. While other basketball players can become flustered by hostile jeers from crowds on the road, Charles Barkley has made the choice to reinterpret the noise by simply telling himself, "They love me!" In her book *Billie Jean,* tennis great Billie Jean King has written that when in competition, "It's like I'm out there by myself . . . I concentrate only on the ball in relationship to the face of my racket, which is a full-time job anyway, since no two balls ever come over the net the same way. I appreciate what my opponent is doing, but in a detached, abstract way, like an observer in the next room. I see her moving to her left or right, but it's almost as though there weren't any real opponent, as though I didn't know—and certainly didn't care—whom I was playing against."

Merging the Physical and the Mental

Remember, there are limits to the amount of improvement that physical training alone can produce. Exercise physiologist Jay Kearney, Ph.D., former director of the sports science and technology division of the U.S. Olympic Training Center, says that elite athletes may spend 1,000 hours of intense, concentrated physical training to improve their performance by just one percentage point. That's a lot of time for a relatively small change. As a result, more athletes are being converted to the value of programs like the Mental Edge.

In the late 1980s a study of 1,200 elite athletes was conducted comparing the training methods of the athletes who competed in the 1988 Olympic Games with those of athletes who qualified for the Olympic trials but didn't make the team. The investigators found many similarities in the physical training techniques of the two groups, as well as in their nutrition and sleep habits. But the athletes who made the Olympic team had spent more time developing the mental aspects of their game, particularly in the hours, days, and weeks before a major competition. That extra effort off the training field made all the difference in the world.

So if you're serious about getting better in your sport, you need to do more than hope or wish for that improvement. The Mental Edge requires an "I want to" attitude as you begin to explore the possibilities that await you. If you have big dreams, you can activate your "superbrain" and ignite the spark of desire into a passionate flame of greater athletic excellence.

This program doesn't require a great amount of time. If you devote just fifteen to twenty minutes a week to the Mental Edge you *will* play better in competition. So as you get ready to begin this plan, ask yourself if you're really willing to "pay the price" to get better in your sport. If you aren't prepared to spend a few minutes each week to make this program work, then it's not your true desire to improve.

You also need to *believe* that improvement is possible. The mind can become a crucial ally, but as you've read, it also can be self-limiting. As long as you truly believe that you can reach your goals, it can happen. The power of belief is real power. It creates a passion that prompts us to willingly pay the price for success.

Research by Maxwell Maltz (the creator of "psycho-cybernetics") has found that our beliefs activate the subconscious processes that can either enslave us or serve us. The subconscious mind prompts us to act in accordance with the "truth" as we see it, based on our conditioned beliefs. Many of these beliefs date back to childhood, and whether they are true or false, they become real if we accept them. Imagine the grade-schooler who is chosen last for the baseball team at every recess, and is always put in right field. He starts thinking, "I'm no good; I was picked last again." When he comes to bat, he ruminates, "I can't hit the ball. Let me strike out quickly and get back on the bench." Those kinds of beliefs and insecurities can linger into and throughout adulthood, convincing us that we are "no good"—in sports and perhaps other aspects of life.

Oftentimes, however, the limits that weigh us down can be conquered with a new mind-set. For example, I find Roger Bannister's achievement of running the first sub-four-minute mile particularly intriguing. Bannister was a physician, and in the years before his historic race articles had appeared in medical journals proclaiming that the shattering of the four-minute barrier was physiologically impossible. Bannister was even warned that he might die trying. Many runners conceded that the four-minute barrier was impenetrable; one of them (John Landy) described it as a "brick wall." But Bannister refused to make these statements part of his belief system, and he eventually exploded past the finish line in 3:59.4, becoming the first runner to break through the mythical barrier.

So what happened next? The belief system of the world's other elite runners changed overnight. Within the next twelve months four other runners also ran sub-four-minute miles; hundreds, perhaps thousands, of others have followed them across the finish line. No longer did runners believe that they "couldn't." And once their thinking was transformed, so, too, was the speed at which they were able to run.

Once you shed your own self-defeating beliefs and everything "clicks," the research shows that you can achieve excellence in sports. Joe Greene, the defensive lineman for the Pittsburgh Steelers, has described the joy of "playing with every part of yourself." In the book *The Winner's Edge: What the All-Pros Say About Success*, sportswriter Bob Oates Jr., quotes Greene as saying that this sensation is "beautiful. You are going all out. You are full of the desire to succeed. You are full of a feeling of power. . . . You reach a peak in every part of your being. You reach an emotional high, a physical high, all of them together. It's almost like being possessed."

The Mental Edge will help you become "possessed," and compete in your sport at levels you never thought possible.

three

Perception Stretchers

Have you ever competed in a sporting event and just *knew* that you didn't have a chance to win? Maybe you believed that you just didn't possess the athletic skills to compete. Or that you weren't tall enough or strong enough. In essence, you gave up mentally before the first shot was taken or the first ball was pitched.

When people tell me stories like this (and they do so often), I sometimes think of "Muggsy" Bogues, the 5-foot-3-inch point guard for the Golden State Warriors. In a sport of giants, Muggsy is the smallest player in the history of the NBA. As you might expect, before he had proven himself as one of the assist and steal leaders in professional basketball, people told him to give up—that he was too small, it was hopeless, he'd never make it.

Almost everyone counted Muggsy out—except Muggsy. He believed that playing basketball wasn't about height. It was as much about heart and desire as anything else. Playing in college at Wake Forest University, he ignored it when opposing fans taunted, yelling "Stand Up!" or when the bands from other colleges played "Short People" as he was introduced. Instead, he stretched his perception of his own capabilities to far beyond what others were willing to do.

In his autobiography, Muggsy put it this way: "I've always been the shortest guy on the court, so I have no idea how a seven-footer sees the game. I only know that the ball's on the floor more than it's in the air. And down there is Muggsyland. That's where I rule."

What a great attitude! He stretched himself to excel in the land of the giants! With an outlook like his, no wonder Muggsy can intimidate athletes who are nearly two feet taller than he.

Too often, however, athletes at all levels of sports think in ways that, in effect, sabotage their performance before they ever set foot on the athletic field. Their attitude is their real problem. They're just not willing to use their mind to stretch themselves to their maximum capabilities. And that kind of thinking can undermine everything that their bodies have been trained to do.

In this chapter I'll introduce you to the Ten Perception Stretchers. They will help you change your thinking about what you can accomplish in sports, despite what you and others may have believed about limitations and shortcomings. They will warm you up for what's to come, expand your vision, and help you prepare for athletic success. By integrating these Perception Stretchers into the Mental Edge program, you'll alter your thinking and develop a frame of mind to take full advantage of the techniques you'll find later in this book.

Let's look at these Perception Stretchers one by one:

1. A loss becomes a gain.

There are few feelings in sports worse than not performing up to your own expectations. Perhaps you compete regularly in a community tennis tournament, occasionally even winning a division title, but unexpectedly you were eliminated in an early round this year. Or maybe you run the mile on your high school or college track team, but opponents whom you once beat easily are now overtaking you in the home stretch.

These scenarios can be frustrating and discouraging. But don't despair. You can learn from these experiences and use them as springboards to improve your performance the next time you compete. Rather than looking at "failures" as major disappointments (which they very well could be), turn the loss into a gain, using it as motivation to change your way of training and thinking in order to enhance your chances of future success. Carefully evaluate how you played that tennis match or ran that race. Were there things you did that interfered with your ability to perform at your peak? Do you need to train differently, eat differently, or think differently to raise your performance to the next level?

In the 1988 Olympic Games in Seoul, American swimmer Matt Biondi was favored to win the gold medal in his first race, the 200-meter freestyle. But at the finish line, he ended up with a bronze, outraced by Duncan Armstrong of Australia, who set a world's record in the process. Two days later, Biondi came up short again, this time in the 100-meter butterfly, winning a silver but losing the race to Anthony Nesty of Suriname by a hairbreadth—0.01 second on the stopwatch.

When Biondi climbed out of the pool after those races, his spirits could have been crushed. But he became determined to turn his losses into gains. He had more events to swim, and so he and his coach huddled, dissecting his second- and third-place finishes, looking for clues hidden within those "defeats." Replaying the freestyle race in his mind, Biondi pictured his pushoff from the starting platform, his first stroke, his turn, and his sprint toward the finish line. Then he used that feedback to plan subtle changes in his upcoming races. He began to visualize how he would feel when he touched the wall at the finish line, ahead of all his competitors.

Biondi didn't pout. He didn't get angry. He didn't become despondent. Instead he carefully examined his previous performances and made some adjustments—and they paid off. He won the 100-meter freestyle in 48.63 seconds, a new Olympic record. Two days later he upset West Germany's Michael Gross in the 50-meter freestyle, winning the gold and setting a world record of 22.14 seconds. Then he raced the final leg of three relay races for the U.S. team, winning the gold—and setting new world records—every time. Not bad for someone whose spirits could have been shattered just a few days earlier.

Even with his early disappointments, Matt Biondi ended up winning seven medals in seven events—five gold, one silver, and one bronze. It was one of the most extraordinary performances in Olympic swimming history.

What should you do when you haven't competed as well as you had hoped? Ask yourself what you could have done differently. There will be something. Examine your attitude, preparation time, and pregame warmup. The seeds of a nonwinning performance may be sown before you even begin to play. What can you draw from the "losing" performance to help you do better next time? You're human, so you're not going to perform perfectly every time. (Remember, Babe Ruth struck out 1,330 times on his way to hitting 714 home runs.) On the one hand, you can let your setbacks get you down, and leave you feeling hopeless and helpless; on the other hand, if you're willing to grow from your "failures," they won't be failures at all. In fact, these so-called failures are important components of the learning process. Sure, it's not pleasant or enjoyable to double-fault your way through an important tennis match, or to double-bogey on the eighteenth hole. But if you regroup, reflect on what's happened, and keep it in perspective, you can use it as a constructive guide toward improving your performance in the next practice and the next match. Think of these disappointments as a way to learn more about yourself and the best way to play your sport.

2. If you do what you've always done, you'll get what you've always gotten.

For many athletes, their egos are much too involved in their performance. As a result, they stubbornly resist making any changes, refusing to admit that there might be a better way to practice or to play. But, in fact, both the mind and the muscles grow through stimulation and by doing things differently and better.

Be an experimenter. Become an innovator. If you find yourself in a rut, rather than thinking about quitting, say to yourself, "I don't like the results I'm getting. What do I need to do differently?"

I sometimes remind athletes of the biblical phrase that we reap what we sow. Well, if you don't like what you're reaping, it's time to sow something new. Maybe you need to change your training schedule. Perhaps the content of your workouts requires an overhaul. Or you might decide to look for a new coach, or even take a break to help avoid burnout. The world's top athletes are always searching for ways to improve, and so should you.

Troy Tanner was an all-American volleyball player at Pepperdine University and a member of the U.S. Olympic team that captured the men's volleyball gold medal in 1988 with an impressive victory over the Soviet Union. After the Olympics, Troy made the switch to two-man beach volleyball, but it was a rocky transition. At times, he didn't play well, and he nursed one injury after another that kept him from reaching his potential. His self-confidence became more fragile, and he began to wonder if he could really compete on the world-class level. He recognized that he needed to make some changes.

That's when Troy started working with me on the mental side of his game, as well as changing his training routine to improve his movement and first-step quickness. Troy and I spent time evaluating his self-perception and belief system. He had been worrying too much about what others were thinking of him and whether he could really make the grade, which undermined his concentration. He agreed to try the techniques presented in this book, particularly performance cues and visualization. And as his training took on these new elements, his game improved dramatically. He had his most successful season ever, finishing seventh on the beach volleyball tour and picking up sponsors and prize money along the way. He had his first injury-free season ever, and perhaps best of all, he had fun training and competing. All because he was willing to try something different. If you try something new, you may re-discover the joy in your game.

3. The imagination is more powerful than the will.

How creative do you feel? I encourage each one of my athlete-clients to tap into their own creativity and apply it to their physical training and competition.

Dick Fosbury was one of America's best high jumpers, and certainly its most innovative. Very early in his career Fosbury jumped like all of his peers, using a technique called the "straddle"—taking off on the foot nearest the bar and swinging the outside leg up and over, with his abdomen and face toward the pit as he cleared the bar. But Fosbury was seeking ways to leap to new heights, although he never could have guessed that his efforts would revolutionize his sport. His will could take him only so far, and so he called upon his imagination to help him soar higher.

At age sixteen, Fosbury started experimenting with a new way of jumping. He began approaching the bar straight on, turning at the last moment and taking off on the outside foot; he left the ground with his back to the bar, and cleared it with his back parallel to the pit, landing on his shoulders and back.

To track-and-field purists, Fosbury was something of a heretic. But he continued to perfect his unorthodox technique while he competed at Oregon State University. Then, in 1968, he used what some sportswriters called the "backward flip" to set a new Olympic high jump record of 7 feet 4¼ inches! At that point no one could say that Fosbury was a flop! In fact, since the early 1970s, virtually every high jumper—from high school to the world-class level—has used what is now called the "Fosbury flop." Imagination had literally lifted Dick Fosbury to new heights.

Many other athletes have used their imagination in one way or another to maximize their inherent physical skills. When playing golf, for example, why not use your imagination in harmony with your body in order to improve your game? Jack Nicklaus, one of the most successful professional golfers in the history of the sport, perceives the mental side of golf, particularly visualization, as 50 percent of his game. In his book, *Golf My Way*, here is how he described the process of using his imagination:

> I never hit a shot, not even in practice, without having a very sharp, in-focus picture of it in my head. It's like a color movie. First I "see" the ball where I want it to finish, nice and white and sitting up high on the bright green grass. Then the scene quickly changes, and I "see" the ball going there: its path, trajectory, and shape, even its behavior on landing. Then there's a sort of fade-out, and the next scene shows me making the kind of swing that will turn the previous images into reality. . . . I believe a few moments of movie-making might work some small miracles in your game.

4. Bodies work perfectly; the mind gets in the way.

You need to let your body function in the way in which it already knows how to work. That means analyzing less, and just letting things happen. If you've trained properly, both physically and mentally, your body will perform up to its potential if you step back and let it "do its thing."

In 1996, in the NBA playoffs, Nick Anderson of the Orlando Magic went to the foul line four times in the final moments of the game, shooting free throws that could have won the game for his team and boosted the Magic's chances of making it to the championship series. Ordinarily Anderson could have sunk the shots almost blindfolded. After all, he was an 80 percent free-throw shooter, and with the ability to come through in the clutch, Orlando couldn't have hoped for anyone better on the line.

But Anderson unexpectedly missed the first shot. As he set up for the second one, he began thinking about how important this shot was—and he missed again. When he was fouled one more time, he went to the line for a third shot, and you could see trouble in his eyes. His expression was taut. He gritted his teeth. His body posture became tense. Not surprisingly, he missed the third shot. As he set up for the fourth, no one expected the ball to find its way through the hoop. In fact, the shot barely hit the basket. Anderson had lost his confidence, and the Magic lost the game.

Anderson's story is a classic example of the mind getting in the way of the body. Over the course of the season Anderson had proven that he was a good free-throw shooter. But he became "psyched out" at the line that night and his body betrayed him. Anderson became the prototype of "paralysis by analysis."

If Nick Anderson had been a student of the Mental Edge, he would have had the ability to relax on cue—not "forcing" himself to relax, but just allowing it to happen. In a relaxed state, he could have shot each one of those free throws just the way he had fired them up in practice earlier that same day, in a frame of mind conducive to success. He could have blocked out the crowd noise. He could have extinguished the anxiety that's often part of a big game situation and sought refuge in a sea of calmness that would have allowed him to shoot naturally and accurately.

Just how important is it to get your mind out of the way so your body can perform? When you're first learning a new athletic skill, you need to fully involve *both* body and mind in mastering the unfamiliar technique. But brain-activity studies of athletes at Arizona State University have shown that peak performance—like that which would occur during competition—is associated with a quieting of the left side of the brain (the hemisphere that specializes in language and logic). By the time you're ready to compete, the body should know precisely what it's supposed to do, and the left brain can take a break.

Timothy Gallwey, whose books such as the *Inner Game of Tennis* have helped many people to "let go" during competition, described the process this way:

> When a tennis player is "on his game," he's not thinking about how, when, or even where to hit the ball. He's not *trying* to hit the ball, and after the shot he doesn't think about how badly or how well he made contact. The ball seems to be hit through an automatic process that doesn't require thought.

The mental preparation you'll learn through the Mental Edge program will help you to free up your body to perform at its peak.

5. Limitations are temporary.

Throughout life we are constantly growing, reaching peaks, and leveling off. But as frustrating as plateaus and apparent limitations may be in sports, they can become a launching pad to the next level of achievement.

Athletes at all levels often find themselves "stuck," feeling as though they can't break through to a faster time in the 100-meter dash or to an extra 5 yards of distance in their field-goal kicking, or beat the person above them on the tennis ladder. Often the stumbling blocks are self-imposed, and the solutions are internal (remember the example in chapter 1 of pole vaulter Dean Starkey and his difficulty in clearing 19 feet). If you find yourself trapped beneath a seemingly impenetrable glass ceiling, desire is your greatest ally. You have to love what you're doing and have a genuine passion to go beyond where you find yourself. The key is to approach each obstacle to your progress as a challenge rather than a brick wall. Instead of saying "Why can't I get unstuck? What's wrong with me?" you need to develop an almost childlike intrigue that asks, "How far can I go? What can I accomplish?"

Mike Powell was an outstanding college long jumper at the University of California at Irvine but seemed to have reached his limit at 28½ feet. He couldn't seem to break through and felt stuck, unable to jump any farther. He decided that he wasn't going to settle for that distance, however. He had the desire to go farther and was willing to sacrifice to get there. Powell changed his workouts. He began using weight machines that stretched and strengthened the muscles used in jumping. He also started a mental-training program, which helped him channel his emotions in a positive way during competition.

At the world track-and-field championships in Tokyo in August 1991, in a showdown with Carl Lewis, Powell's commitment paid off. He had lost to Lewis in fifteen previous meets, and he became so anxious before his initial jump that evening that he had trouble breathing. None of his first four jumps was memorable. But once he calmed himself down, Powell soared into the night of his life. On his fifth jump, oblivious of the threatening storm clouds overhead, he rocketed to a new world record—29 feet 4½ inches—surpassing Bob Beamon's long-standing mark by 2 inches. After the meet Powell revealed that he had been picturing himself breaking Beamon's record. "I've been dreaming about this for two years," he said.

Occasionally your own physical limitations may be against you. For example, if you want to be a jockey, but you're the size of Shaquille O'Neal, the best mental attitude in the world isn't going to help. But for most people, apparent barriers shouldn't be looked on as "insurmountable." Think back to the story of Muggsy Bogues. The first time he showed up at the athletic dormitory at Wake Forest University, other players thought he was someone's little brother. At 5 feet 3 inches, Muggsy could have quit trying to play basketball. Instead he did what he had to do to succeed, finding ways to compensate for his physical "limitations." Basketball, he said, is "not a game for peo-

ple who are big. It's a game for people who can play." And
Muggsy has always played like he is seven-feet tall.

6. Anyone can play any sport better.

Every athlete wants to improve, but most don't know
how. One effective technique for playing better is to pattern the excellence of others. Select an outstanding athlete
who performs the way you want to, and break down his
or her skills into mini-steps that will create a pattern for
you to follow when you play. Then use visualization and
imagination to develop a better performance by seeing
yourself exactly the way you want to be. If you become
more like your role model, you'll play your sport better.

Let's say you're a baseball player and you want to hit
better and feel more confident at the plate. Get started by
finding a player whom you'd like to pattern yourself after,
perhaps Tony Gwynn or Ken Griffey Jr. Then watch how
he approaches the on-deck circle. Observe the way he prepares himself before stepping into the batter's box. Study
his stance from head to toe. Evaluate his swing. Look at
how he responds when he hits a line drive into the gap.
Watch how he sprints down the line toward first and
rounds the bag toward second. In short, step into your role
model's skin, and as you do, you'll become more like him
or her.

My daughter is a member of her high school track and
volleyball teams and her role model is Misty May, one of
the best setters in college volleyball, who plays for California State University at Long Beach. She has watched
Misty play many times, and I've told her, "Act like Misty

May. Think like Misty May." She has patterned her playing on May, and her game has improved.

Bill Russell, the Boston Celtics basketball legend, began this process when he was still in high school—and not only on the basketball court. His first career goal was to be an architect, and he used to study the works of Michelangelo and try to reproduce them. He started using the same technique for basketball while playing on a high school all-star team. He began studying the moves of Eural McKelvey, one of the players on the team, particularly the way McKelvey would grab an offensive rebound and muscle his way up for a shot. Russell played and replayed that image of McKelvey in his mind. Finally he started letting those images direct his own performance in game situations.

"When I went into the game, I grabbed an offensive rebound and put it into the basket just the way McKelvey did," Russell recalled in his autobiography, *Second Wind*. "It seemed natural, almost as if I were just stepping into a film and following the signs. When the imitation worked and the ball went in, I could barely contain myself. . . . [F]or the first time I had transferred something from my head to my body."

7. Events have no meaning except what you give them.

If you've ever found yourself in a crucial situation in a pivotal game—perhaps batting with the bases loaded, with two outs in the ninth—you can probably still feel the lump in your throat and the weakness in your knees. Any time you experience a situation like this—brimming with pressure—you're likely to be distracted and you probably won't hit as well as you otherwise would.

In circumstances like this, despite the nerves or "butterflies," you need to remember that a baseball game is just a baseball game, whether it's in a community league or the World Series. The basics are the same—pitching, hitting, throwing, catching, sliding. Nothing really changes except the meaning we give it. We are the ones who pressurize the situation by mentally approaching it in a different way. The pressure comes only from within.

Of course setting aside that tension isn't always easy. Just ask the world's elite athletes, most of whom still have to battle to keep their attention on the competition itself. In the minutes preceding the 100-meter race at the 1988 Olympics, Carl Lewis's focus was drifting, and he had to keep reminding himself to just run his race. "Seconds before getting in the blocks, I lost my focus again, thinking about all the pressure, the thousands of people in the stadium and billions watching on television," he wrote in *Inside Track*. "I wondered if I wanted to do this anymore. Luckily, these thoughts didn't last long, maybe ten seconds, but the gun was less than a minute away. Something clicked, and I was able to snap out of it. Just run your race. Focus."

Anxiety is *not* a tangible thing floating in the air around you. It's something that *you* create internally. While you might think that stress is an inevitable part of sports, you can learn to eliminate it as quickly as you've created it, or use it to play better. Superstars like Reggie Jackson, Magic Johnson, Chris Evert, and Jerry West raised their performance levels a notch when they were in pressure-packed game situations.

As part of the Mental Edge, you'll begin to enjoy the process of competition again. You'll become more child-like and focus on and relish the moment. You'll acquire a mind-set that allows you to maximize your sports performance no matter what the circumstances. Even in a situation that may seem pressure-packed, you can allow your body to work perfectly, without fear of being attacked by what can become your worst enemy—you.

8. Getting better is more important than winning.

Too many people focus on Vince Lombardi's famous pronouncement that "winning isn't everything; it's the only thing." In fact, an emphasis on winning limits you, and cheats you of some your potential. I've even seen it lead to self-destructive behaviors, from anabolic steroid abuse to the illegal doctoring of high school or college grade transcripts.

Instead, your goal should be to perform at a peak level. From Little League diamonds to Yankee Stadium, from Pop Warner fields to the Rose Bowl, many athletes never reach their potential because they're overly concerned with winning. They actually shoot their careers in the foot because they're not focused on getting better. Their emphasis is solely on winning, and that takes the fun out of the game.

Pole vaulter Dean Starkey has competed on the world-class level for years, but as these words are being written, he has never beaten Sergey Bubka of the Ukraine, perhaps the greatest vaulter of all time. If Starkey's sole focus were on winning, he might become hopelessly discouraged and stop training altogether. But he continues to work hard, knowing that if he performs better—if he can vault just a little higher than before—he'll enjoy vaulting more. To Dean, there is more to sports than winning.

Walter Payton, the great Chicago Bears running back, once said that his biggest fear was not living up to his potential. So he kept his focus on getting better and becoming his best. It was that mind-set that produced his NFL rushing records. Of course Payton wanted to win. Everyone does. You can't win all the time, but you can always work on becoming better. And as you do, winning will take care of itself.

9. Practice like you play.

Some genetically gifted athletes are just born to perform in the top 5 percent of competitors in their sport. They sometimes can get away with not practicing hard, and they'll still play well. They won't become their absolute best this way, but they'll still enjoy some marvelous achievements.

The rest of us, however, need to work a lot more intensively. When we're out on the training field, practicing hour after hour, we're relying on our brains to establish and strengthen connections between mind, body, and emotions and create memories that can be called upon during competition. For that reason you need to practice the way you want to perform, because that's the way you *will* perform.

If you're a golfer, for example, you need to do more than spend most of your time on the driving range. Yes, you may learn to drive the ball perfectly in that environment, but you won't play enough rounds on an eighteen-hole course to learn to hit the ball over and around the trees and the sand traps that can sabotage your game.

Some basketball players concentrate primarily on playing the half-court game during practices. It's much less exhausting, and maybe some of them are a little lazy. They aren't, however, preparing their bodies, minds, and emotions for an actual full-court game situation. They aren't practicing like they need to play. As a result, practice never makes perfect, but rather it makes for something far less. No wonder many great half-court players can't make the transition to the full-court game. The focus and intensity you bring to your practices will reward you on game day.

10. The more you expect from a situation, the more you will achieve.

This is what I call the "high-expectancy performance" theory. If your team is behind in the fourth quarter, but you and your teammates fully expect to rally back, you'll play better than if you're just trying to hang on. A bowler who expects to hit the 1-3 pocket in the tenth frame and is eagerly waiting for his turn to do so will outperform an opponent who is simply stepping onto the alley and hoping to keep the ball out of the gutter.

Do you remember Kirk Gibson's heroic home run for the Los Angeles Dodgers in the 1988 World Series? Hobbled by knee injuries, Gibson wasn't expected to play, but he pinch-hit in the bottom of the ninth, with two outs and his team trailing 4–3. On a full count (three balls, two

THE TEN PERCEPTION STRETCHERS

1. A loss becomes a gain.
2. If you do what you've always done, you'll get what you've always gotten.
3. The imagination is more powerful than the will.
4. Bodies work perfectly; the mind gets in the way.
5. Limitations are temporary.
6. Anyone can play any sport better.
7. Events have no meaning except what you give them.
8. Getting better is more important than winning.
9. Practice like you play.
10. The more you expect from a situation, the more you will achieve.

strikes), Gibson set aside the pain and the pressure, and rather than saying, "Oh God, it's up to me!" he told himself, "I live for these moments. I'm going to make contact." He fully expected to hit the ball solidly, despite his physical pain—and he did. Focusing solely on the ball, he blasted the pitch into the right-field bleachers. He limped around the bases to give the Dodgers an unforgettable victory in one of the greatest moments in World Series history.

Modest expectations tend to produce modest results. I've known volleyball coaches, players, and parents who simply don't anticipate a good performance for morning matches. And invariably they don't do well. But if other teams play up to their potential, why can't everyone? Limited expectations have probably impaired the way some athletes play.

When you focus on the possibility of real success, however, your senses will become sharper, your enthusiasm levels will soar, memories of achievement will trigger your muscles into their highest levels of activity, and you'll take another step toward realizing your potential.

Reread the Ten Perception Stretchers frequently. They'll help you stretch to achieve your maximum performance.

Defining Your Desire

Great achievements don't start with reality. They start with desire.

In sports, desire needs to be more than hoping or wishing for success on the tennis court or the golf course. It is really a dominating dream—so dominating, in fact, that your inner strength and commitment become focused on turning that desire into reality.

In this chapter I'll guide you toward creating your own Desire Statement—a definitive description of your athletic goal(s)—which will become an important element in helping you reach your dreams. This statement might be "I want to improve my golf handicap from a five to a three." Or "I want to improve my three-point shooting accuracy from 30 percent to 40 percent." Or "I want to be able to pinpoint my pitches to hit corners of the plate." An important step in transforming these wishes into reality involves putting the desires down on paper, which is a clear, concrete way of saying "This is what I'm going to do. This is what I'm committed to."

Just like small fires create small amounts of heat, weak desires generate weak results. But when a powerful Desire Statement transforms that small fire into a raging inferno, it can put you on the fast track toward accomplishing your athletic goals. It will produce an "I want to" attitude that is so intense that it dramatically increases the likelihood of dreams becoming real.

The National Hockey League, in collaboration with coach Terry Orlick, Ph.D., conducted a study to determine why some players reach the NHL, while most do not. Scouts and coaches were asked about the qualities that separated those who make it to the pros and those who don't. Of the characteristics cited repeatedly, desire was among those at the top of the list. Desire, along with determination, attitude, heart, and self-motivation, were the qualities that set the outstanding hockey players apart from the also-rans. You'll notice that skating ability, checking, and shooting weren't the characteristics that made the difference.

The Power of the Desire Statement

When Emmitt Smith, the great running back for the Dallas Cowboys, was playing in high school in Florida, his coach told him, "It's a dream until you write it down. Then it's a goal." In subsequent years Smith put his desires into writing, revising them when appropriate. In 1993 he wrote down his dream of breaking Walter Payton's all-time NFL rushing record, and what he would have to do to turn that desire into a reality—averaging 125 yards rushing per game, avoiding fumbles, and staying healthy. In an article in *Sports Illustrated,* he said, "I can be there, but I've got to hit one helluva pace. . . . I can do that."

If you've never created a Desire Statement you might wonder how it can affect an athlete's performance. If you were to write down "I want to lead the soccer league in goals this year" or "I want to have the best earned run average on my team," how does that translate into kicking or throwing the ball better?

When athletes can create clear mental pictures—perhaps images of themselves winning a mile race or sinking a 25-foot putt—they are creating a connection between their mind and body, providing a blueprint that allows the body to perform better during actual competition. Desires activate subconscious processes that begin to work automatically to improve sports performance. They create opportunities to take us beyond where we had been before. Obstacles don't disappear, but they become negotiable hurdles that we are able to go over, through, or around.

Later in this chapter, when you create your own Desire Statement, don't hesitate to think big. Big desires cause the brain to think big and learn new skills quickly. The mind tends to move toward our dominant thoughts, and if your Desire Statement is strong and compelling, you will activate the brain to move beyond conventional thinking, and trigger subtle physiological activity that can help turn a desire into a reality.

In working with athletes at all levels, I've found that many had only vague, nebulous goals, with no strong commitment to them. They have told me things like "I'd love to play golf better," "I want to be a pro someday," or "I'd like to win a college athletic scholarship." But once they think through those desires a little more clearly, and define them better and write them down, they feel like they've made giant strides toward making those same goals tangible and attainable.

There have been about 400 studies on goal setting in sports, and about 90 percent of them have found value in the process. On average, according to the research, athletes can improve their performance by 8 to 16 percent just by setting goals. And since winning and losing is often determined by a fraction of a second, or by a shot at the buzzer that swishes through the hoop, a 16 percent improvement can be dramatic. If your Desire Statement is important enough for you to make a strong commitment to it—that is, for you to decide that you'll do whatever it takes to make your desire come true—it can become a powerful motivator that allows you to pursue your goals aggressively.

Jack Youngblood, one of the greatest players in Los Angeles Rams history, had a clear Desire Statement that motivated him throughout his football career: "I want to play in the Super Bowl." His desire was so strong that he refused to let anything interfere with his dream. In fact he even played in the championship playoffs with a fractured leg! He was accustomed to playing in pain, and a little more discomfort than usual wasn't going to sabotage his goal.

Youngblood said the following about desire: "You learn that whatever you are doing in life, obstacles don't matter very much. Pain or other circumstances can be there, but if you want to do a job bad enough, you'll find a way to get it done." And he did.

Do You Believe in Yourself?

Jack Youngblood believed in himself. But many athletes aren't brimming with that much self-confidence—a fact that can get in the way of creating a Desire Statement, and of bringing it to reality.

As I wrote earlier in the book, beliefs activate the sub-conscious processes that can either enslave you or serve you. Your beliefs can unleash your talents to achieve greater heights; or they can undermine your dreams and cripple your efforts, keeping you from giving 100 percent. To write a meaningful Desire Statement you need to free yourself from any limitations that you have placed on yourself.

Negative beliefs are created in many ways. They can be influenced by events of the past—a missed putt on the eighteenth green, an errant field-goal attempt on the final play of the game, or a comment by a coach or a parent. Some of them may even date back to grade school, when you might have been picked last as baseball teams were being chosen. That painful experience can linger well into adulthood, with subconscious thoughts like "I'm no good; everyone knows I can't play well" or "Why should I start a workout program? I'll never get in shape." Once these beliefs become ingrained in our subconscious—even if they have no basis in reality—they become real for us, and weaken our confidence each time we step onto the athletic field.

Take a moment to try this exercise. In the space below, write down a limiting belief—at least one, but no more than two—that you have of yourself as an athlete.

_____

_____

_____

_____

Next ask yourself the following question: "What irrefutable evidence exists that this belief is true?" There probably is none. You may find that this belief—that you can't pitch a baseball with any skill, or that you can't drive a golf ball accurately—is not true, or is at least exaggerated. Remember, anyone can do anything better—maybe not world-class, but better.

Because we tend to perform consistently with our beliefs, those self-defeating beliefs must be changed so that they support our Desire Statement. Beliefs can be reshaped and altered. In fact, the limits we place on ourselves are nothing more than our own failure to exercise our imagination and change what we believe. As neurologist Richard Restak has said, reality is not so much constructed as created. And you can begin to create the reality you want for yourself.

This process may involve little more than *choosing* new beliefs that will help make you the athlete you imagine. Give up those self-limiting beliefs, in the same way that, at some point, you stopped believing in Santa Claus or the Tooth Fairy. Athletes I have worked with have told themselves, "I'm better than that," "I've proven that I can play well under pressure," or "The athlete I was in the past will not determine who I will become in the future." Even though you may not be performing at the level you want to—for example, if you aren't yet consistently kicking 40-yard field goals—you need to believe that it is possible (which it probably is!).

If Tom Dempsey had a different belief system, he might have been watching football from the grandstands rather than playing it. He was born with a partial right arm and only half a right foot—his kicking foot—and he seemed like an unlikely candidate to become one of the greatest field-goal kickers in NFL history. Unlikely to everyone, perhaps, except Dempsey. He believed in himself despite his physical challenges. And so, beginning in high school, he spent hour after hour practicing his kicking while wearing a custom-made shoe. Dempsey rose to the ranks of professional football, and while kicking for the New Orleans Saints, he made sports history. In a game with the Detroit Lions in 1970, with just two seconds remaining on the clock, he kicked a 63-yard field goal through the uprights—the longest field goal ever—lifting the Saints to a 19–17 victory and proving that his "limitations" weren't real.

Take a few moments now to write down five *positive* beliefs that you have about yourself. Think about it, and you might be surprised by what you come up with. Perhaps you have the self-discipline to practice with greater intensity than you ever did in the past. Or your hard work may have improved your acceleration out of the starting blocks in the 100-meter dash. Your statements can be very brief; my son, for example, has responded, "I'm strong . . . I'm fast . . . I'm smart."

Write down your own positive beliefs:

1. _____
2. _____
3. _____
4. _____
5. _____

Now take a moment to read these beliefs aloud. Read them with emotion and feeling. As you do, acknowledge that they are preparing your mind and body for greater performances in the future. Brains and bodies learn quickly. Without a doubt, your level of success in sports (and in life) will rise as your self-concept improves.

As long as your mind can envision your attainment of new heights, you are most of the way there. Belief can create a passion to motivate you to fulfill your desires.

Creating Your Desire Statement

It's time to write a Desire Statement. Give it some thought, and then put your primary goal as an athlete into writing. It can be a lengthy sentence or, if you wish, several sentences. Make it as simple or as detailed as you like.

Your Desire Statement might be "I want to throw strikes." Or it could be a little more detailed: "I want to throw strikes at ninety miles per hour that are unhittable on the outer edge of the plate."

The Desire Statement must be motivating for you. It needs to be the kind of statement that, as you read it over and over, turns your desire into a passion. For some people their statement might be "I want to run faster." For others it could be "I want to run a four-minute mile before I finish my college career, and compete in the Olympic Trials in the year 2000." One athlete wrote, "I want to run the New York Marathon, and end up among the top fifty finishers."

Write your Desire Statement below. Dream a little. Stretch yourself.

_____

_____

_____

Keep the Desire Statement positive. Unfortunately, some people seem attracted instinctively to the negative. Their Desire Statement might be: "Don't strike out anymore!" or "Run faster so I won't be a loser." That approach does motivate some athletes. But I think you'll gain much more from this exercise by focusing on the positive. Rather than saying "Don't strike out anymore!" create a Desire Statement that says, "Make contact with the ball, and hit more line drives." Instead of writing "I don't want to slow down along the backstretch of the 400-meter run," change it to "I want to accelerate through the backstretch of the 400-meter run."

There is nothing more powerful than a made-up mind. If you commit yourself to your Desire Statement you will move in the direction of this dominant thought when you play your sport. Write the Desire Statement every morning and every night for the next ten days. Even though you already know what it says, putting it down on paper again and again will help reinforce it. Read it each time with enthusiasm and belief. Keep the desire in the forefront of your mind. It's also okay to change the statement a little, or a lot, with time. As your performance changes, or circumstances change, you can adjust your Desire Statement accordingly. Feel free to let it grow, take on new meaning, and become more real.

If you're like most people, the more detailed your Desire Statement, the more enticing it will become. One way to expand upon it is to define the benefits and rewards that will accompany the realization of your desire. You can pair your Desire Statement with a Reward Statement. For example, by making the track team of your high school, or by winning the tournament at the local bowling alley, what rewards will you reap? The prospect of a coveted reward will increase your motivation to make your Desire Statement come true.

In one of the earlier examples, the baseball pitcher might expand upon his original Desire Statement, which was "I want to throw strikes at ninety miles per hour that are unhittable on the outer edge of the plate." He could add a Reward Statement that proclaims, "By doing so I can become first team all-league and be in the running for a college athletic scholarship to Stanford so I can get a college education, which my parents really can't afford."

Your own Reward Statement should be unique and motivating to you. If your Desire Statement is to win a gold medal in the Olympic Games, what will you achieve as a result? The exhilaration of being the best you can be? Celebrity status? Commercial endorsements?

One of the athletes I work with wants to play professional football. His Reward Statement has two elements: "A pro career will give me a comfortable lifestyle; it also will allow me to serve as a role model for kids and show them that if they work hard to reach their own dreams it can happen for them, too." A marathon runner has a Reward Statement that says, "By running I'll stay in shape, keep my weight under control, and look better." A swimmer aiming for the Olympics developed a Reward Statement reminding himself that making it to the Olympics would allow him to live out a childhood dream of representing the United States in international competition.

During those tough training days, when you'd rather quit early than go the extra mile, your Reward Statement can help you to persevere. Your training will take on an entirely new dimension once you can see the payoff that will accompany running a little faster or jumping a little higher.

Write down your Desire Statement again, and then add a Reward Statement to it:

DESIRE STATEMENT: _____

_____

_____

REWARD STATEMENT: _____

_____

_____

By going through this process you will improve more quickly, regardless of the level at which you are starting.

Creating an Action Plan

Now that you've produced your Desire Statement and Reward Statement it's time for the next step. You need to write down the physical and mental training program you must adopt to make these two statements come true. Look at the reality of your present situation—that is, your current speed, quickness, discipline, and so on—and determine what's necessary to reach your dream. What do you need to do during your training—on the field, in the weight room, and on the mental side? Then put the answer to these questions in writing in an Action Plan.

I believe that the Action Plan is essential for most athletes, even those blessed with obvious innate talent. Catcher Mike Piazza was not drafted by the Los Angeles Dodgers until the sixty-second round, and his chances of ever making the major leagues were slim. But Piazza committed himself to a program that would develop his skills to their fullest potential. As he worked his way through the minor leagues, he spent extra time in the weight room, the batting cages, and behind the plate digging pitches out of the dirt. He might have believed in himself from the start, but unless he had become committed to a plan of action, he never would have developed into one of the best baseball players of his time.

Of course not every successful athlete has had a clear plan of what he or she needs to do to attain a higher level of achievement. Some do well with just the most basic idea of what it takes to excel during their sports career, pushed along by a dream so compelling that they just "have to make it happen." Most of the athletes I know—both professional and amateur—have found that a concrete plan pinned on a bulletin board or attached to the refrigerator door helps them commit to the program and realize their Desire Statement more quickly.

Not long ago I worked with a high school basketball player whose Desire Statement simply said, "I want to earn a college basketball scholarship." I asked him to get more specific: Where did he want to go to college? A Division I, II, or III college? Did he have a particular school in mind? After giving it some thought he set his sights on the University of Michigan. Although he was a talented athlete, he realized that he still had a lot of work to do to get to a point where the Michigan basketball coach (or coaches from other colleges with great basketball traditions) would notice him. So he created an Action Plan that would transform him into a top recruit.

"I need to become stronger and faster, and jump

higher," he told me. So as part of his Action Plan we developed a workout routine that would improve these skills. It included a weight program and jump training three times a week, and speed training twice a week. He changed his diet, adding more protein and cutting out the candy bars that he once kept in his backpack. He added mental training to his Action Plan, too. As this is being written, he is a sophomore dunking about mid-forearm-high. "I believe in myself, and I'm never going to quit," he told me.

In your own Action Plan, create a detailed program for yourself. There are three areas you need to examine in making an Action Plan: How do you think? How do you eat? How do you train? To explore these areas, you might ask yourself questions such as:

- "Do I have the attitude of a champion?"

- "Do I believe in myself in the midst of adversity?"

- "Am I letting other people affect my thinking?"

- "Am I eating to maximize my performance?"

- "Do I use the latest training techniques?"

- "Do I consume too much junk food?"

- "Am I maximizing my training?"

Based on the answers to questions like these, you can create a detailed program for yourself addressing the specific shortcomings you've identified. How many days a week will you practice, and what are your goals each day? What will you include in your workout plan? Will you seek outside coaching? What mental training techniques will you use, and how many minutes a day will you spend practicing them? How will you adjust your diet, and will you include any food supplements?

Use the space below to create your Action Plan. Make it as detailed as possible, but keep in mind that it is always subject to revision as your skill level improves.

MY ACTION PLAN IS: _____
_____
_____
_____
_____
_____
_____
_____

Are You Willing to Pay the Price?

I've always loved beach volleyball. I still play it today, years after I began competing in the sport. When I was in my twenties I even considered playing on the professional two-on-two beach volleyball circuit. It was a dream of mine, and I knew I'd have a great time.

But I also realized that I'd have to pay the price of becoming good enough to compete on the pro tour. I acknowledged that I'd have to make a much greater time commitment—both on and off the beach—to develop the skills to become good enough to play professionally. I knew how talented the pros were, and I wasn't at that level yet. I saw the kind of effort they put forth. I knew how hard they worked out. I also believed that I could do it; genetically, I had a good start, with a vertical jump in the mid-thirties (inches, that is) and a very quick first step. With the right physical and mental training program it was possible. But frankly I wasn't willing to pay the price. Realizing that my business needed my attention, and that I had commitments to my family that I was unwilling to ignore, I decided to stay just where I was—playing level 3 beach volleyball, light years removed from the pro circuit.

Looking at your own Action Plan, are you willing to pay the price to adopt it in full? If you aren't, then your Desire Statement probably isn't as strong as you think. It may be a wish. It could be a hope. But a halfhearted effort won't make it come true. Yes, your Reward Statement may be very seductive. But the Action Plan tells you definitively what the price of achieving that reward will be. You must decide whether you're willing to pay it.

I worked with a young baseball player not long ago whose talents were above average. His Desire Statement was to play major-league baseball someday. But he was not willing to spend the time working to improve his speed and strength, nor to commit to a mental training program. As a result, he remained just where he was—a very good line-drive hitter, but without power and with unimpressive speed. He still hoped to play professional baseball, but he wouldn't go into the weight room, devote time to running drills, or change his diet from junk food to a healthy eating plan. That left his Desire Statement hollow, and unlikely ever to become a reality.

Some people have real problems implementing their Action Plan, suffering lapses in their work ethic when they realize how hard it is sometimes to climb to the next level of achievement. In certain cases athletes become discouraged with the frustrations that are an inevitable part of the process (you may have been the best player on your high school squad, but you'll start out as just one of the pack on the college team). Other times, after an enthusiastic start, athletes decide that the pain (physical and/or mental) is just too great to endure to reach their goal. They may no longer have the self-discipline to stick to a new training schedule or diet regimen. So they give up and never reach their full potential.

In a sense the level of passion to succeed parallels the reaction of people who have been stranded in the wilderness. Some of them, even those having had survival training, see their situation as bleak; their brains shut down, they stop looking for ways to survive, and they never make it out alive. But other people, with the same training and in the same circumstances, tell themselves, "There's no way I'm going to die. I'm going to find a way." And they do. Driven by their passion to survive, they discover a way out of the wilderness. You can do the same on the athletic field.

In a study of the Swedish national badminton team, its members were asked what separated them from their fellow athletes who were not selected for the team. Repeatedly they answered that their commitment was greater. They "wanted it more" than their peers. They were willing to train harder. They never surrendered, giving 100 percent in practices and competition. They pushed themselves, even when their exhaustion levels were high. They rose to the challenge, paid the price, and as a result, enjoyed success.

Ben Hogan, the great golfer, was renowned for his commitment to whatever it took to excel at his sport. Nothing gave him greater satisfaction than hitting a golf ball, and he rarely passed up opportunities to hit a few more—and often more than a few. His practices included hitting up to 1,000 balls over a five- to six-hour period.

In his book, *My Partner, Ben Hogan,* golfer Jimmy Demaret recalls Hogan shooting a record 64, including ten birdies, in the opening round of the Rochester Open. After the round Demaret and most of his fellow golfers finished the day by socializing over drinks in the clubhouse. But Hogan went to the practice tee instead, where Demaret spotted him hitting wood shots into the night.

"What are you trying to do, man?" Demaret asked him. "You had ten birdies today. Why, the officials are still inside talking about it. They're thinking of putting a limit on you!"

Hogan looked at his friend and said, "You know, Jimmy, if a man can shoot ten birdies, there's no reason he can't shoot eighteen. Why can't you birdie every hole on the course?"

Hogan had set the bar as high as it would go. And it is obvious he was willing to pay the price to clear it.

The Value of Mind-Setting

To a large degree your desire and beliefs will determine how far you will go in sports. With proper mind-setting you can lock on to your goals and keep your self-confidence and enthusiasm levels high. If your Desire Statement is specific and attainable, it can activate all of your mind's thinking processes to teach you new skills quickly.

Through goal setting and mind-setting, you can take the Desire Statement that proclaims "I want to," to the achievement state of "I will." Too many people operate with an "I'm not sure" attitude that leads to partial effort, and almost inevitably, to disappointment.

Most people—in and out of athletics—go through life wishing and hoping for the best; but it takes more than that to realize your dreams. Concrete goals are a crucial element in the road to success. A study of Yale University graduates found that only 3 percent of the class of 1953 had written down clear, specific goals for themselves. Twenty years later, those 3 percent had greater financial worth than the entire remaining 97 percent. With a commitment to achieving their personal goals, they also reported greater satisfaction in life.

When Doug Nordquist was twelve years old he watched the Olympics on television and became intrigued with the high jump. Dwight Stones, the great high jumper, instantly became Doug's idol, and Doug wanted to be just like him. So Nordquist committed himself to that goal, and began practicing with the determination to let nothing get in his way. Over a period of years Nordquist gradually refined his high-jumping skills. He practiced in bad weather. He jumped despite injuries. His mind was focused on the prize. Nothing would stop him.

Doug Nordquist not only became a world-class high jumper, but he eventually beat his idol, Dwight Stones, in head-to-head competition. He was able to keep going because of a strong desire and an unwavering mind-set.

Being *Smart*

When you are working on mind-setting, the acronym SMART will help you with the process:

Specific: Create a Desire Statement and Action Plan that are as specific as possible. Make it clear precisely what you want to accomplish. You're better off saying "I will shoot 90 percent from the free-throw line," than "I'd like to become a better free-throw shooter." With the clearest possible statement, your mind can call upon the resources you need to achieve what you want.

Measureable: Keep track of your improvement, which will motivate you to keep going. If you're starting out as a 70 percent free thrower and you want to get to 90 percent, monitor your progress . . . from 70 to 75 to 80 percent and up. This information will show you that you're on the right track.

Attainable: Your goal needs to be a reachable one, meaning that you must be willing to pay the price to get there. If you're unwilling to make the necessary sacrifices—for example, to practice shooting free throws for thirty to sixty minutes a day—you may not have the mindset to fulfill your Desire Statement.

Realistic: Shooting free throws at 90 percent is achievable. But if you set your goal at 100 percent, that's probably a Mission Impossible. How can you tell if your goal is realistic? Ask yourself if anyone has achieved it before. Evaluate your present talents—both strengths and weaknesses—and compare them to athletes who have already attained what you want to accomplish. But keep in mind

Roger Bannister's achievement. You may be the first and break a barrier.

Time: Set a time frame in which you want to turn your desire into reality. If you're trying to go from 70 percent to 90 percent at the free-throw line, you may need an entire season (or maybe more) to get there. Create a time line and keep your mind focused so it expects to reach the goal in that time frame.

As you progress, allow yourself to be driven by your Desire Statement and Reward Statement. See the future that you want. Then work backward, picturing yourself overcoming the obstacles in your path. And along the way enjoy the process of striving toward your desire.

five

A Picture of Excellence

When Lee Evans trained for the 400-meter race in the 1968 Olympics, he did more than run revolution after revolution around the track with the stopwatch ticking. He also spent many hours quietly visualizing the race as he would run it in the Olympics, and how his body would perform from beginning to end. He imagined every stride he would take, one after another. As he did, his actual running form gradually improved, and so did his times. In Mexico City he not only won a gold medal, but he set both an Olympic and a world record (43.8 seconds) that lasted twenty-three years before it was finally broken.

Was Lee Evans doing anything particularly unique? Not really. Most of us visualize all the time, both in and out of athletics. Before falling asleep we may run through our mind what's likely to happen during an important meeting at work the next day. Upon awakening we may picture the dozen or so tasks we must go through—from cooking breakfast to dropping the kids off at school—before leaving for the office. Many times during the morning, afternoon, and evening we might "daydream" about events or circumstances in our lives, picturing how they will play out.

In the Mental Edge Program this visualization (or imagery) is much more formal. It is a process in which you will call upon all of your senses to prepare you mentally for your sports workouts and competition. In your mind you will play and replay the precise experiences you have (or want to have) in your sport, including the exact movements your body makes. These three-dimensional, multisensory images can become one of your most powerful allies in your athletic career.

In his book *In Pursuit of Excellence* coach Terry Orlick related the story of how members of the national archery team used visualization to get ready for competition:

> A former world champion spoke of how, through imagery, she was able to transport herself to the world championship from her practice site. Instead of seeing the single target that was actually in front of her, she saw targets stretched across the field. She was fully aware of her competitors. On her right was the leading Polish archer, on her left a German. She could see them, hear them, and feel them. She shot her rounds under these conditions in the same sequence as she would shoot in the real competition. She prepared herself for the competition and distractions by creating the world championships in imagery and by actually shooting under mentally simulated world championship conditions.

How Does Visualization Work?

A growing body of research has shown that the combination of visualization and physical training helps enhance on-the-field performance better than physical workouts alone for both recreational and professional athletics. Here is some background on how this imagery works:

The brain has two hemispheres, and you use both of them all of the time. The left hemisphere utilizes logic and analysis; it is very verbal, tapping into words to relate to the world. During visualization, however, you rely much more on the right hemisphere, which is responsible for imagination and visual pictures. As you create images you are actually linking both hemispheres and using all of the tools available to you to help make your athletic performances as good as they can be.

Researchers have discovered that, in a real sense, visualization puts your body through the paces before you ever walk onto the athletic field. Vivid images can produce subtle but real firings along the neural pathways that participate in the physical activities that you are visualizing. For example, in a study published in the journal *Behavior Therapy*, researchers tracked the EMG muscle activity in the legs of skiers who were visualizing a downhill run; the electrical activity in their muscles mirrored what occurs during actual skiing. Similar findings have been observed in athletes in many other sports, from basketball to weight lifting to karate.

During visualization you are essentially "priming" the muscles for the particular task ahead, whether it is to improve your free-throw shooting or hit a spin on the ice rink. You condition your brain, nervous system, and body to perform in the way you want it to, thus increasing your chances of doing well in competition. It helps create self-confidence. And it puts your brain and body in a comfort zone that allows you to perform well when the moment of competition finally arrives.

Mental Edge Visualization

Let's get a taste of visualization. Start by thinking back to your Desire Statement. Ask yourself again what your desire is in athletics. Is there an athletic goal that you'd like to achieve? In the following visualization exercise you will experience yourself being there now, as though you had already achieved that outcome:

▪ FUTURE PACE ▪

Close your eyes, take a deep breath, exhale gently, and pretend it's a time in the future. It's a moment when you've achieved a fitness or sports goal that you've sought for yourself. Perhaps it's running a 5-kilometer race in under twenty minutes. Or maybe it's hitting drives on the golf course straight and true, and farther than you've ever done before. Develop an image in your mind of the goal you're striving toward, and the day it becomes reality. . . .

As you imagine yourself in this setting, having already achieved your goal, notice the expression you have on your face. Perhaps it's an ear-to-ear smile. Or a calm, relaxed picture of contentment. Spend a moment getting in touch with that image. . . .

Next, notice your body posture. Is there an air

of confidence to your physical presence? Are you standing tall with your shoulders back? How are you breathing?

Also, what are you thinking now that you've achieved your goal, now that your dream has become real? And how are the people around you reacting? How does your achievement make them feel? Experience their words of encouragement, the pats on the back, the high fives. . . .

As you enjoy the rewards of your physical accomplishment, ask yourself, "Was it worth it? Was it worth the dedication and the commitment that got me here?" And as you conclude that it was, start to work backward in time. Notice some of the obstacles you had to overcome along the way to achieve your goal. . . . Notice the negative people with whom you had to contend, those who had once said that you were as good as you would ever be, that you were already playing to your potential. . . . Observe some of the beliefs about yourself and your capabilities that you had to change. . . . Pay attention to how serious you became about your goal.

Continue to work back in time, and examine where you had been months or years earlier when you had just begun this quest. Notice how far you've come in this relatively short period of time. Allow yourself to experience satisfaction over what you've accomplished.

Just before opening your eyes, feel good about allowing your whole mind, your entire body, and all your emotions to work together in harmony to make this happen.

This exercise has put you into the future, allowed you to experience what your success will be like, and shown you what led up to that achievement. It gives your mind a path to follow. It can be a powerful exercise, but it is only one way in which visualization can be used.

Priming Yourself for Peak Performance

Perhaps the most powerful use of imagery is to prepare you to perform to your maximum ability, particularly in the heat of competition. It can be used to improve your performance in virtually every athletic situation. For example, try the following exercise:

Sit quietly in a comfortable chair and close your eyes. With your body and mind still, and with your breathing relaxed, allow images of your athletic performance to enter your mind. Picture yourself going through the motions of the skill that you're trying to perfect. Imagine every move, even the tiniest details.

If you're a golfer, for example, see yourself standing at the tee. . . . Picture your backswing . . . your shoulder and hip turns . . . the arm movements as the club approaches the golf ball. Check your posture and how it changes as you perform. See the golf ball bounding onto the green and rolling into the hole. . . . Notice the expression on your face as it does. At the same time, hear the sounds around you . . . the purr of the golf carts nearby, the chatter of the other golfers.

Become aware of your feelings of pride and excitement with your success. Listen to what you're saying to yourself, and experience the feelings of accomplishment that begin to overwhelm you.

Now, let's take this exercise to the next step:

There are six knobs in front of you. They can help you adjust and enhance your visualization experience.

Reach for the first knob, and use it to adjust your internal "zoom lens" to make the imaginary picture larger. See how it completely covers your mind's screen; it is three-dimensional and vivid. . . .

Now reach for the next knob. As you turn it, enjoy the enhancement of the colors in your picture. Watch them become so vivid that you can't help thinking, "Wow, this is great!" . . .

Then add a little brightness. The picture is becoming more brilliant as you do. . . . Next turn up the volume. Make your images loud but still comfortable, alluring but not ear-shattering. . . .

Now adjust the tone. Fine-tune the sound so it is sharper and clearer than ever before. . . .

Finally, replay these images over and over. Study them. Absorb them. Enjoy them.

Got the idea? The key is to make your images as clear, detailed, and vivid as you can. Maximize your senses. Use everything at your disposal to make the most of your visualization. For example, if you're working on images related to football competition, make sure you cover everything—the bright green color and smell of the grass on the field . . . the vivid white chalk of the sideline markings . . . the taste and the coolness of the Gatorade you drink on the sidelines . . . the sensations of the football helmet as you place it over your head . . . the wind blowing on your face . . . the feel of the mud on your fingertips as you crouch at the line of scrimmage . . . the sensations of the football nestling into your chest as you unexpectedly intercept a pass . . . the exhilaration you feel running the interception toward the goal line, bouncing off blockers . . . and the voices and facial expressions of the players you're competing with and against.

Don't leave anything out. On a scale of 1 to 10, sharpen your images from a 6 to a 7, then to 8, 9, and 10. As you approach and reach these 10's, this exercise will become increasingly productive. Later you'll step onto the field with greater self-confidence. At the same time, your body will model these images when you're actually competing.

Some Real-Life Examples

Most world-class athletes use visualization. Before they ever step into the starting blocks or walk out to the pitcher's mound they have experienced what that competitive situation will be like—seeing it, hearing it, feeling it, smelling it, and tasting it, down to the smallest detail. They work with visualization so often and so intensively that their bodies eventually know everything that they are capable of accomplishing, and just how to do it.

Nick Bell, a running back for the Oakland Raiders, spent a few minutes visualizing before going to sleep every night. He pictured himself finding holes on the line of scrimmage, breaking tackles, and crossing the goal line. Freeman McNeil, the all-pro running back for the New York Jets, credited visualization for much of his football success. He said, "Sometimes I'll be running off of pure instinct, following whatever my subconscious sees." He became very skilled at creating such vivid images that he could eventually trust his body to perform just as he had visualized it. And Dwight Stones, the Olympic high jumper whom I've talked to in researching his technique, became known for his mental rehearsal before each jump; his head bobbed in a rhythm coinciding with the visual pictures he was creating of himself running toward and leaping over the bar.

Amateur triathlete Tom Skultitley proved himself to be one of the best visualizers in athletics as he trained for his first Ironman triathlon in Hawaii, perhaps the most grueling challenge in sports. He had decided that not only did he want to compete in the Hawaiian event, he wanted to end up among the top ten finishers, and cross the finish line in under ten hours.

Not surprisingly, Tom placed himself on a rigorous physical training regimen. But that wasn't all. At the same time, visualization became an important training tool for him. Day after day he pictured himself swimming, cycling, and running the race, with his wife embracing him at the finish line, and the pride and ecstasy he felt in accomplishing his goal—in the top ten, and under ten hours. He could sense the smile enveloping his face, and the handshakes and the pats on the back from his fellow athletes.

Then Tom would visualize himself training, and he'd fill in all the details . . . the rigorous demands of swimming, cycling, and jogging. Yes, he could feel the pain, but at the same time he found joy in the sensations of a finely tuned body functioning at a level of near perfection. He could hear his feet kicking in the ocean . . . see the tires of his bicycle speed over the pavement . . . sense the perspiration drenching him from head to toe in the final miles of the marathon. He pictured the magnificent Hawaiian scenery along the triathlon route, including the stark black images of the scorching hot lava fields. He used those sharp, inspiring images to motivate him during the long, hard days of training. As Tom trained in Omaha in January, with an outdoor temperature of 20 degrees, and a 20-mile-an-hour wind in his face, he could call upon those vivid pictures to keep him motivated. When other athletes were finding excuses to skip the day's training session, he rarely missed a workout.

As the months passed, Tom went from visualizing a little and training a lot to finding a greater balance between the two. In the week before the race he visualized four hours a day! In great detail he would see, feel, taste, smell, and hear everything he possibly could about the upcoming competition. At the same time, he never lost sight of the outcome that he wanted; his image of crossing that finish line in Hawaii, exhausted but excited, never wavered.

When Tom finally competed in the Ironman, he swam,

cycled, and ran it just the way he had visualized it. Even though he did not wear a wristwatch, he completed the race in 9 hours, 59 minutes, and 37 seconds—breaking his target time by less than half a minute. He finished ninth, the highest ranking of any amateur. For Tom, visualization had clearly worked.

Refining Your Visualization Skills

Although the word "*visua*lization" suggests that sight is the only sense used in this process, you've read how the other senses—hearing, smell, touch, and taste—are just as important in this performance-enhancing technique. As you practice imagery you need to concentrate on using all of your senses in order to experience the moment fully, as though it were really happening now. If you're having difficulty making or keeping your images vivid, use those six knobs in front of you that control your images. Remember, they influence brightness, size, color, volume, tone, and the intensity of your feelings.

Go back to the Future Pace exercise (page 80). Take a few moments to recapture the image that you had created of where you'd like to be athletically at some point in the future. Now, in your mind's eye, take control of those knobs. If you're a swimmer, imagine yourself feeling the cool water engulf your body as you dive into the pool . . . the strength of your kick and arm movements, stroke after stroke . . . the smell of the chlorine in the water . . . the sound of the crowd cheering you on to victory.

As you use all of your senses and increase their intensity your imagery will tend to become more *associated* than *dissociated*—that is, you will become completely involved in the pictures in your mind, fully experiencing them as though they were really happening to *you,* and happening *now.*

As you practice visualization in the weeks ahead, pay attention to whether you're visualizing in this associated way. Are you fully in the movie, immersed with all of your senses in the action? Or are you seeing a movie in which someone else appears to be starring? Dissociated visualizing has some value as a learning tool for studying the nuances of a sport. For instance, if you're working on improving your stride while sprinting, a dissociated image can help you see what you look like running today and can help you evaluate your own form; it's as though you're an observer in the grandstands or a coach on the sidelines watching yourself run. Then, once you've seen what you need to do, step back *fully* into the picture, and through visualization, begin to feel what it would be like for *you* to run at your peak. As your imagery becomes stronger your body will actually begin to experience the micromusclar movements that can program it to run better.

Let's say, for example, that you're a weekend tennis player who wants to improve your crosscourt backhand. As a first step, think for a few minutes about what you want to achieve. Then ask yourself, "How far away am I from that goal?" To help answer this question, use dissociated visualization to clearly see where you are.

Next, switch your visualization to an associated state, where you are involved completely in the images. The pictures in your mind should concentrate on what it would look like, feel like, sound like, smell like, and taste like to make perfect contact with the tennis ball in a backhand stroke. Picture the ball speeding over the net and landing exactly where you want it to go.

Frankly, the biggest mistake that most people who teach visualization make is that they don't encourage their student-athletes to move from the dissociated to the associated state. In fact they never bother to distinguish between the two. As a result, many visualizers see their images as if they're happening to someone else. They may even see themselves sitting in the stands watching themselves run. Thus visualization never becomes the powerful tool for them that it could be.

Make It a Positive Picture

Throughout visualization keep your images positive. For example, picture yourself jumping over the hurdles on the track, not knocking them over. See yourself hitting a solid line drive to the outfield, not swinging and missing the pitch. The images you visualize are likely to come true, so make sure that these pictures are the ones you want to become part of your reality, including the skill levels you want to achieve.

Many great athletes have appreciated the enormous power of the mental images they've created. In the 1988 Olympics in Seoul, after Greg Louganis struck the back of his head on the diving board during a qualifying round, he refused to watch a video of the mishap, fearing that he would subconsciously create a powerful negative picture in his mind that could undermine his diving in the finals.

Louganis explained, "I didn't want that image in my head going into the competition." So instead, with five stitches in his skull, he concentrated on making perfect dives—and won gold medals in both the 3-meter springboard and the 10-meter platform.

Troubleshooting Your Visualization Problems

Sometimes I hear athletes say that they've tried visualization and it doesn't work. They claim that they "don't have the patience for it," or that they "haven't got the creativity or the imagination to make it work." In fact, *everyone* can visualize and reap benefits from it. Some people simply have more trouble than others getting the process started.

If you're visualizing in a dissociated state (seeing the images in a detached manner rather than being intimately involved in the activity), your pictures may be vague, fuzzy, and unclear. You may have difficulty imagining the sounds, smells, tastes, and touches that surround the pictures you've created. And that will keep you from activating the neural pathways between mind and body and experiencing the micromusclar movements that can translate into improved performance on the athletic field.

If you're having difficulty, begin asking yourself questions such as "What have my positive experiences on the athletic field sounded like?" . . . "What did I see?" . . . "What did I hear?" . . . "What did I smell?" . . . "What did I touch?" In the first few sessions, don't be overly concerned about clarity and detail. They will develop over time as your images become stronger. Remember, most people think that visualization involves only the visual sense, but you really need the participation of *all* of your senses for this technique to work.

Visualization does take practice, so even if you're having difficulty at first, don't give up. When you're practicing, pick out an object in your room, study it, and then close your eyes and try to see it; getting a sense of it can send powerful messages to the brain. Some athletes break through their obstacles by starting out with an image of a single sports-related object, perhaps a basketball. They picture everything about it, from the way it looks to the way it feels to the way it sounds when it bounces. As they work with those images and make them sharper, they then begin to expand them beyond the ball to the entire basketball court, and develop images of themselves fully involved in the game—shooting jump shots and blocking shots.

Your use of visualization can't be halfhearted. It needs to become an integral part of your athletic training. Just like a soccer player needs to practice physically kicking dozens of balls toward the goal every day, he should also be practicing his visualization exercises as well.

To get the most out your visualization sessions keep these guidelines in mind:

· Know exactly what you want to accomplish before you start. In your visualization, allow yourself to feel as though you've already achieved your goal.

· Keep your imagery personal, positive, detailed, and in the present.

· Experience all of the emotions and feelings that you possibly can. Keep all the images associated—that is, as if they are happening to *you*.

· Don't force it. Your subconscious mind will guide your body to perform like the athlete you see in your mind. You should practice visualization, but let your brain and body do the work.

· Don't expect instant results. Perform visualization once in the morning and once at night. Be patient and your skills will improve.

· Don't expect visualization to compensate for a lackadaisical approach to your physical training; if you're a golfer, you need to hit buckets of golf balls as well as visualizing the act of hitting them.

· Before a game or a competition, run through your visualization exercise, reviewing what you want to accomplish.

There's no denying that visualization can have a dramatic impact on your athletic performance. Consider Greg Maddux, for instance, who was a struggling pitcher with the Chicago Cubs, with earned run averages of 5.52 and 5.61 in his first two years in the major leagues. He didn't have an overpowering fastball, nor a curve that consistently fooled batters. He also had a reputation for letting his emotions run wild on the mound.

But then Maddux began developing the Mental Edge

and learned to prepare himself mentally before games. Maddux began to visualize his success, one pitch at a time. He started to vary the speed of his pitches and developed pinpoint accuracy in hitting corners of the strike zone.

By working on both the psychological and physical sides of his game he began to improve quickly and dramatically. In fact, with the Cubs and later the Atlanta Braves, he became one of the greatest pitchers in the history of baseball. He won the Cy Young Award four consecutive years in the 1990s and almost certainly has a place in the Hall of Fame waiting for him.

If you want to become a great athlete, you should work at becoming a great visualizer. Give it a try. I believe you'll find that engaging your mind is as important as engaging your body.

A Visualization Worksheet

As you practice visualization, use the worksheet below to keep track of how you're doing. I suggest filling out a form like this after your first visualization session, and then about every two weeks thereafter as you continue to practice the technique.

My visualization goals are: _____

_____

_____

When I practice visualization, my experience is: _____

_____

_____
_____

I do well in the following area(s): _____
_____
_____
_____

I can improve in the following area(s): _____
_____
_____
_____

My athletic performance is changing in the following
ways: _____
_____
_____
_____

six

Building on
Your Own Success

All people who play sports, whether they participate just for the fun of it or for a world's record, dream of attaining what I call the Maximum Athletic Performance State (or MAPS). It's the moment when everything clicks. They perform better than they ever have, entering what many of them call "the zone"—a mental state so focused and intense that it evokes a semiconscious-like euphoria that facilitates peak performance. When they pitch, they seem to be throwing aspirin; when they bat, the baseball looks as big as a volleyball. When they hit an off-balance tennis backhand, it moves across the net with more power, more top spin, and more accuracy than it ever has. Everything happens perfectly and almost effortlessly.

You have the power to move yourself to MAPS, reaching your peak performance level, and it won't require pushing yourself to the point of exhaustion on the tennis court or the ice skating rink to get there. You've begun to integrate mental conditioning techniques into your sports training program; in the process, you've taken giant strides toward creating harmony between your mind and body. In this chapter we'll discuss other techniques—including the Success History Search and Performance Cues—that can keep you focused on winning in the heat of competition.

The Power of Consistent Resilient Action

Motivation can be fickle. In fact research shows that motivation lasts an average of about seventeen days. Almost inevitably, your enthusiasm will wane with time, unless you do something to keep your eye on the prize.

To work on motivation, I urge my clients to take Consistent Resilient Action, or CRA. It is really nothing more than action pursued by a made-up mind—an internal drive that creates excitement and commitment and never lets up. Through mind-setting, you can develop enthusiasm and passion for a game plan—e.g., a training schedule, a workout routine—that you can stick with no matter what. It's really a matter of never losing sight of your Desire Statement, reading it often (for some people that means every day), and sticking to the course that you've charted.

So take a moment to renew your commitment to your Desire Statement, the one you created in chapter 4. Make sure that you never lose sight of it. Become tenacious and follow through.

MY DESIRE STATEMENT IS: _____

_____

_____

You need desire in order to develop the drive to reach your goals. But not everyone has a desire strong enough to develop a powerful, internal drive; they have more of a wish than a true desire. When the desire is real, however, and it is the focus of your attention and energy, it will become your dominant thought and can push you toward achieving your goal.

Just how far can desire take you? Just consider the story of basketball great Larry Bird. He was a good high school player, yet he never seemed destined to become one of pro basketball's great superstars. Bird enrolled at Indiana University, but wondered if he'd ever get the chance to play (seven players on Indiana's 1974–75 team would make it to the NBA). He said he didn't feel comfortable there, and couldn't motivate himself. So he dropped out of school before playing even a single game for Indiana, and he hitchhiked home. His mother was devastated, lamenting to her friends, "What's he going to turn out to be? A bum?"

But Bird had never lost his love of basketball and the underlying belief in his ability to play. He worked in his uncle's gas station for a while, and then collected trash and mowed lawns. Finally he came back to the courts at Indiana State University, and although he certainly had talent, he had developed something more—the commitment to succeed in his new college environment. Almost immediately he began turning heads. As Bird wrote in his autobiography, *Drive,* "Here I had gone from a high school player who had dropped out of college to a guy who made third-team All-American in his first year."

Once he turned pro, Larry Bird's enthusiasm never wavered. Even though some players were faster and could jump higher, he believed in himself. "When I first came up, all I thought about was establishing myself as a professional, to prove that I *wasn't* too slow and all the other things my critics said I was—or wasn't," wrote Bird. He added, "I always worried that I couldn't run and couldn't jump," so he worked instead to perfect his shooting and passing, and boxing opponents off the boards. Obviously his hard work paid off.

Many other athletes have shown this same Consistent Resilient Action. Runner Mary Decker was more injury-prone than most athletes. But with each injury, she only recommitted herself to excelling once she was back on the track. She trained tirelessly and consistently. When she fell during the 1984 Olympics, she showed her resilience by bouncing back and returning to her training routine. She kept going, and she kept getting better, and she was still competing on the world-class level in the late 1990s.

Jon Lugbill had the same unshakable constitution. He was a kayaker and a five-time world champion. His desire was so strong and uncompromising that *nothing* ever interfered with his workouts. Inclement weather, from rain to snow, never kept him indoors. When his kayak was being jostled by blustery winds, he considered it part of the challenge. His belief in himself was so powerful, and his mind was so locked into his desire to succeed, that he was never tempted to come in from the cold. While his peers were looking for excuses to skip a day of training, he would look for reasons to keep going—and going and going.

What about you? CRA can compensate for most shortcomings in your talent. If you're willing to work harder and stick to your physical and mental training program, you'll enjoy more success than you ever dreamed possible. When others are still in bed waiting for their alarm clocks to ring, you'll already be on the training field. While they're watching television, you'll be practicing visualization. Even if you weren't blessed with the best genetics, you can bless yourself with desire, determination, drive—and success.

It's much easier to achieve once you believe that you can. And, in fact, all of your sports and fitness goals are within reach.

Tapping into Your History of Success

Throughout this book I have emphasized and reemphasized just how important your mind is. With mental training you can become the athlete you picture yourself to be. Before you step into the batter's box for your softball team, if you imagine yourself blasting a line drive over the third baseman's head, you have a much greater likelihood of hitting one there than if you picture yourself dribbling a ground ball to the first baseman. Remember, imagine yourself the way you want to be.

It's also important to set your sights high. The more you expect from yourself, the more you will achieve. For instance, if your team is behind in the game, but you and your teammates expect to rally back, you'll always play better than a team just trying to hang on. An ice skater who approaches a competition expecting to hit all of her jumps is more likely to skate flawlessly than if she "just doesn't want to mess up." Modest expectations produce modest results. But when you focus on the possibility of real success, your enthusiasm peaks, your senses become sharper, and memories of success remind your muscles of actions that work. As this happens, you'll take a quantum leap closer to reaching your potential. At the same time, if you maintain this high expectancy, you'll recover quickly

when setbacks do occur and be ready almost instantaneously to stretch yourself again toward your goals.

Success History Search

An important tool in this process is the Success History Search. It allows you to focus your mind on past successes to prepare you for future achievements. It can
rescue you from shaky self-confidence and send an unde-
niable signal to the body that says "I can! I will! I am!" It
uses your mind to empower your body to perform to its
capabilities.

If you feel overwhelmed or anxious when faced with a
long putt, you're probably focusing on the possibility of
failure, perhaps unconsciously. But the Success History
Search teaches your brain to concentrate on images, feelings, sounds, emotions, and thoughts of success, providing
you with a foundation for performing well in the face of
difficulty or fear and giving your mind a winning course to
run on.

Let's walk through the Success History Search together:

Let yourself relax and then close your eyes.
Think of a time in the recent past when you felt
good about accomplishing something. It may be a
day when you performed particularly well in a
sporting event. Or it can be an achievement at
school or in the business world. Perhaps it was
something you accomplished even though you had
doubts that you could. It might have been the first

time you broke par in a round of golf; or maybe it was the day you closed a big business deal, or got an "A" on a chemistry test in college. Everyone has an experience like this that he or she can call upon. It could have happened yesterday, or ten or more years ago, but the clearer it is in your mind, the better. Whatever personal achievement you choose, paint a vivid picture of it in your mind's eye, and allow yourself to feel really good about yourself and what you accomplished. Take a few moments to enjoy those feelings. . . .

To help you get more completely in touch with this positive experience of the past, notice what kinds of thoughts are running through your head as you immerse yourself in this successful experience. . . . Pay attention to what you are saying to yourself and what others are saying to you. What sounds are you hearing around you? What are you seeing? What expression is on your face? What is your body posture like? Allow these images and sensations to become more intense, penetrating, and embellished. Experience all of your senses as fully as possible. Allow yourself to feel good about the experience. Enjoy the moment and let it continue for at least two or three minutes. . . .

Next, think of an even earlier time when you experienced feelings of success and accomplishment. Concentrate on an achievement in sports, school, or business. Maybe it was something you were initially a little fearful about even trying, but later, after you had succeeded, you felt so good about going for the gold. It gave you confidence

that you could move on to even greater successes. . . . As this event envelops your mind, begin
to experience the feelings and the physical sensations that are part of it. . . . Concentrate on the images of that moment. . . . Relive your internal
dialogue, what you were thinking at the time, as
well as what others were saying to you. . . . Let the
images become more intense. . . . Feel the excitement of the moment. . . . What were the sounds,
sights, tastes, and smells of that experience? . . .
Notice how good they make you feel today, just as
good as they did back then. . . .

Now, one more time, choose still another accomplishment, even further back in your past.
Again, let yourself reexperience that moment . . .
every thought, every emotion, every sight, sound,
and physical sensation. Let it absorb all of your attention. Become more involved with these images
with each passing moment. Enjoy them and give
them some time to become ingrained and rooted in
your unconscious mind. . . .

Finally, take a deep breath and open your eyes.
As you bring this exercise to a close, you may be
surprised that you feel not only relaxed and content, but simultaneously energized with a powerful
sense of well-being and self-confidence.

How did you fare? This Success History Search allows
your mind to embrace feelings of accomplishment. Everyone has had successes in his or her life—and they don't
have to be huge successes. It could be the first time you
completed a pass, or the day the coach told you how well

you made a block to free the fullback to cross the goal line. The key is to recall *everything* that went along with it—all of the sensations, all of the emotions. By reliving positive experiences through strong, vivid images you are speaking the language of the intuitive, instinctive part of your brain. When you communicate directly with this part of your mind, you'll be better able to burst through the glass ceiling that may be limiting your athletic performance.

Use the Success History Search before practice sessions and competition. Each time you do your unconscious mind will build on those past successes and increase your chances of future success. This technique literally reestablishes old connections between body and brain, strengthening memories in the mind and muscles that can be replayed every time you perform. In the weeks ahead, when you're in the midst of a batting slump or are having trouble leaving the gate with power at the top of a ski run, you can call upon these positive images to turn your performance around.

Brains learn best from images, and the more intense—and the more positive—they are, the better. It's crucial to saturate your mind with positive, not negative, images. As I've already stressed, if you walk to the free-throw line right after picturing yourself missing one shot after another, your chances of sinking the shot are negligible. That's why I've called this exercise the *Success* History Search. You don't want to give your mind and body any messages contrary to what you want to have happen; if you do, you'll set up an internal battle that gets in the way of winning.

Imagine what will happen if a manager walks to the mound and tells his pitcher, "Whatever you do, don't throw it high and outside—it's the batter's sweet spot." Well, that's like telling someone not to think of a pink elephant. Almost inevitably the pitcher will start telling himself, again and again, not to throw it high and outside—and his mind will take that image, process it, and *increase* his chances of tossing it right where it shouldn't go. That's what happened to Hall of Fame pitcher Warren Spahn in a World Series game, when he gave up a home run just seconds after he was told where *not* to throw the ball. So keep your images positive.

Of course no one can guarantee that the Success History Search will get results every time. But I've seen it work often and on every level, changing attitude and posture and giving the athlete a better chance to perform at his or her peak. I've watched baseball stars like Tony Gwynn hit a weak grounder back to the pitcher in a crucial situation, but before his next at bat, call upon his mental abilities to put that momentary setback aside; by the time he hits again, he fully expects to get a single—and he often does. I've seen Liz Masakayn, an excellent volleyball player, spike an easy one into the net; but almost instantly, certainly by the next serve, she fully anticipates performing up to her capabilities. With the help of the Success History Search Liz can dismiss mistakes quickly and ready herself for maximum performance.

Sure, John Elway of the Denver Broncos may have been sacked a half dozen times and thrown three interceptions in the first three quarters of a game, but it barely fazes him. He knows that he has pulled out many games—literally dozens of them—in the final few minutes. So when his team is behind in the fourth quarter, he can draw upon his past successes. They get his brain in tune with the belief "Yes, I can do it."

In a sense, the Success History Search is priming your body to perform as it should. It's almost like an actor rehearsing before the opening of a play; over and over, he practices his lines at home, on a tape recorder, in front of a mirror. At times the process may seem tedious, but there is only one opening night, and he knows that it's crucial to be prepared when the curtain rises. In the same way, an athlete needs to be fully ready when she steps onto the soccer field or the track, and thus she needs to use *all* of the "weapons" at her disposal. If you practice the Success History Search, you will find it a powerful component of your mental training program.

Responding to Performance Cues

Next, let's apply the positive input from the Success History Search in another way, using Performance Cues. A cue is really nothing more than a stimulus that elicits a predictable response. You've probably heard of studies by Ivan Pavlov, the Russian psychophysiologist. His experiments with dogs demonstrated the conditioning process. He would ring a bell, show a hungry dog some meat, and, of course, the animal would salivate. After repeating this process many times, Pavlov eliminated the middle step— that is, he rang the bell but didn't show the meat to the dog. But because of the repeated pairing of the bell and the meat, the dog had become conditioned to salivate whenever he heard the bell. The bell became a cue or a sensory stimulus that the dog responded to in a consistent way.

Cues give permanence to an experience. They create certain emotions and feelings within us, even though we're not consciously trying to tap into them. For instance, when a song from the past comes on the radio—perhaps a record by the Beachboys or the Beatles—it automatically takes us back to that special summer with that special person, and we relive that moment in our history—automatically. We think of the past and feel a rush of emotions associated with an experience that may be decades old. In the same way, a former baseball player may smell newly mowed grass and instantly experience a sensory surge that brings him back to the ball field that he played on years before.

Often cues occur outside of our awareness, many times developing by chance. When Monica Seles was the best women's tennis player in the world, she would grunt unconsciously whenever she hit the tennis ball. She did it for years, shot after shot, match after match. Every time her racquet connected with the tennis ball, she grunted. She sounded like a martial artist breaking bricks.

At one point, however, other players complained that the noise was distracting. Bowing to pressure, officials at Wimbledon silenced Monica. At their insistence, she made a conscious effort to remain quiet while playing—and she lost what should have been an easy match.

It was like telling Michael Jordan to keep his tongue in his mouth when he plays basketball. Monica had created a cue that connected grunting and success. Every great shot was accompanied by a grunt. That noise might have started as a way to put more physical strength into her shots; however, it became something more—a crucial stimulus response that, through repetition, became a cue to success. And when she was silenced, she played at a level below her potential.

Not long thereafter, at the U.S. Open, Monica insisted on bringing back the grunting, louder than ever. And she began winning. Years later it took a physical assault by a spectator brandishing a knife to finally put an end to her string of impressive victories and retire her from the pro tennis tour until her return in 1995. Now she's back—and so is her grunting.

Monica is one of many hundreds of great athletes who rely on cueing to help them perform well. Consider the baseball player who steps to the plate. He twists his head left to right. He flexes his right arm like a weight lifter in training. He windmills his bat twice and spits out some sunflower seeds, which land inches from his lucky socks, the ones he wore in the first game of the year when he went four for four. He gently taps the bat on the left side of his helmet as he digs his feet into the batter's box, and then rests his bat on his shoulder. Finally, his cues have been activated, and he's ready for success.

When All-American swimmer Rodrigo Gonzales competed, he would step onto the starting platform, utter the word "Explode!" focus on the black lane lines in front of him, and then reach down and touch the edge of the platform on which he was standing. When he said "Explode!" he could actually see, hear, and feel an explosion! These were the cues that could trigger a conditioned response and lead to maximum performance.

Sometimes cues can be offbeat. I worked with a well-known NFL lineman who wanted to raise the level of his play a notch. He would yell "I'm the man!" and simultaneously grab his crotch for a second or two before taking his stance on the line of scrimmage. For him, this kind of performance cueing has helped him make the big play when it's necessary.

These rituals, which you may have noticed while attending various sporting events, can spell the difference between success and failure for many athletes. In the same way, you can integrate cueing into your own sports performances. I've taught this technique to basketball players on the Seattle Supersonics, baseball players on the Kansas City Royals, football players on the Oakland Raiders, and coaches in the National Hockey League. It has worked for elite athletes and it can make a difference in your own sports achievements, too, even if you're only a weekend athlete more interested in fitness and fun than in winning.

Performance Cues

Here's one way to begin creating a cue for success:

1. With your eyes closed, and in a state of relaxation, formulate an image of a peak sports state from the past. Using the Success History Search, go back in time to a moment when you performed up to your full potential, or very close to it. Relive the physical sensations, the feelings and the emotions associated with that experience. On every level, make it come alive, as if it were happening now. Create images so vivid that it's as though you weren't *watching* your performance, but you were actually *doing* it all over again. Turn up the volume, adjust the tone, and make the colors bright and intense. Then, when the sensations can't get any stronger and more powerful, move on to step 2.

2. Choose a unique Performance Cue to use in this exercise. It could be a word, a gesture, or a ritual. But it must be an unmistakable signal to the brain. The best cues involve sight, sound, feeling, taste, or smell. It might be a word as simple as "Excellent!" "Great!" or "Yes!" Or it might be squeezing your left hand in a unique way, perhaps touching your thumb to your forefinger; or grabbing a knuckle or squeezing your wrist. The only requirement is that it helps you recall the achievement of an earlier experience, which in turn sends a signal to the brain and the body to do what they have to do to support success and winning. Use a word that best describes the feelings you experienced when you performed at your best.

The cue must be something you can consistently call upon and duplicate in a moment. For instance, let's say that you've chosen the word "Excellent!" as a cue. You'd want to say it exactly the same way each and every time you invoke this technique. Or if your cue is clenching your right fist as you recall feelings of your best sports performance, you would want to squeeze it precisely the same way each time.

3. Say your cue word—or perform your cue movement—five times. Do it with intensity. If it has two components—for example, stating the word "Excellent!" and clenching your right fist—take the memory of that past event, imagine placing those images in your right hand, make a fist, and lock that memory in. Pump your fist and say

"Excellent!" five times with passion and conviction.

This cueing technique allows you to stimulate and instantly relive your successes from the past. For instance, when you caught a pass and ran down the sidelines for a touchdown at the company picnic, you did everything you wanted to do. As you relive that experience, put it in your right hand and say your cue word with fervor as you make a fist; like Pavlov's dog, your body will respond instinctively in ways that will increase your chances of achieving another touchdown catch at the next game. When you serve an ace on the tennis court, take that experience, get passionate about it, and squeeze it into your hand; then, the next time you play tennis, let that clenching of your fist alert your body that it's time to perform exactly the way it's capable of doing.

Keep your cue words simple. Forget about anything long and drawn out, like "Hit it sharp and down the third base line!" Instead, follow the guidelines that appeared in *Scientific American* in 1996 in an article on Olympic athletes. It described the training regimen of Tammy Forster, a twenty-seven-year-old shooter who excelled on the rifle range. She not only used relaxation exercises and visualization as part of her training, but she incorporated cues into her program to help her overcome her shaky confidence while competing. These verbal cues were amazingly simple. They were single words, such as "ready" and "relax." And they became part of an overall program that produced impressive results: she won two world cups and finished second in the national championships in her event.

When I play volleyball these days, I use Performance Cues as needed during a match. If I shank a jump serve directed at me and need to get my focus back, I'll immediately turn to cueing; I'll say my cue word ("Yes!") while squeezing my right hand into a fist. I do it with passion and belief. It's my reminder that I can rebound on the next serve, and it helps me maintain my concentration. I don't have to go back and methodically think about all of my past successes because with the Performance Cue I'm keying into them instantly and automatically. Some of these old successes can come from totally unrelated events—perhaps in basketball, triathlons, or rock climbing; but as long as they were challenging, the Performance Cues tied to them carry the message "Bring it on!"

After you've used Performance Cues for a while, try stacking even more elements into them. For example, I often add emotions as well as new physical qualities to my cue. If the cue is clenching my right fist, I'll incorporate a distinct posture, facial expression, demeanor, and feeling that, over time, I will assume whenever my fist squeezes shut. Every time I activate the cue—the clenching of the fist—the accompanying posture, expression, and emotions will help set the stage for an outstanding sports performance, while also sending signals to my brain that will more fully prepare my body for action.

Also, remember to keep your cues positive. Not long ago I worked with a weekend golfer who was stuck on the same score for months. He just wasn't improving, and one reason was his own unconscious sabotage, brought on by *negative* cues (including exclamations such as "Not again!" as his shots sailed into the rough). I had him shift to positive Performance Cues—approaching shots with confident statements such as "Smooth . . . relax," while clenching his left hand as if he were gripping the golf club. Within a month he had lowered his average score by three shots per round.

In the future, when you take to the ice for a skating performance or walk onto the golf course, put your Performance Cue into action with passion and conviction, and you'll experience a flood of thoughts and emotions tied with success. As that happens, you'll give your body the opportunity to perform at its highest possible level.

The Power of "Power Talk"

"I can't hit. . . . I choke under pressure. . . . I'm not an athlete. . . . I never stick to my workouts."

If these are the kinds of statements you're reciting to yourself while you compete, what do you think is going to happen? Of course you're not going to perform at your best. All of us talk to ourselves as we compete and train (and in every other aspect of life), reacting to the obstacles and the opportunities in front of us. The information we gather is filtered through our belief system and becomes our "truth," even if it is not based on fact. We create an inner dialogue based on this information, and if it contains and sends us a negative message ("I choke under pressure!"), it's going to undermine how well we practice and play.

Remember that when self-talk is filled with criticism, and when it reminds us of our limitations, it can destroy our concentration and confidence, create fear and anxiety, and make it harder to perform.

Power Talk is another technique for sending positive messages to your brain and body. It is a way to get beyond negative thoughts and surround yourself with a mental environment of excellence that supports a specific action or outcome. You can use it to condition your mind to focus on your athletic prowess, not on your limitations. It is particularly useful in altering a habit or improving a skill.

Power Talk is quality thinking. It is tied to emotions that eventually displace any negative feelings that you're experiencing. Picture placing a glass of dirty water under a running faucet; eventually, the dirty water will be displaced by clean water, and once the glass is filled with that clean water, there won't be any room left for the dirty. In much the same way, once you fill your mind with Power Talk, there won't be any space for negative thoughts. This technique has the ability to transform your belief system and propel you in a new direction.

Power Talk

Here is how to incorporate Power Talk into your sports program:

1. Determine something in your personal athletic world that you want to change. It may be a characteristic, a behavior, or a skill level.

2. Use the space below to write out an "I am" statement that describes this goal as though you had already accomplished it. For example, a tennis player might simply say, "*I am* a good tennis player." A runner might say,

"*I am* a great finisher." A volleyball player might say, "*I am* a great jump server." A basketball point guard could say, "*I am* a good decision maker on the court." Keep it positive. Keep it in the present tense so it becomes a "here and now" exercise.

I am _____

_____

3. Now refine your statement a little by making it more specific and attaching emotion to it. To help you reshape your statement, answer questions like, "How fast do I want to run?" or "How much weight do I want to lift?"

Here are some sample Power Talk statements:

· "I am a skilled tennis player with a great first serve."

· "I am a great finisher with a strong kick, and can pass anyone at any time."

· "I am a great jump server, and I put it where they ain't!"

· "I am a good decision maker on the court, and always hit the open man!"

Many Power Talk statements have keywords in them. Sam Snead, the great golfer, used the word "oily" in his inner dialogues, which reminded him to keep a fluid swing. Gymnasts often use the word "forward" to reinforce the need to push themselves ahead at certain moments in their routines.

Although you want to set goals for yourself that require you to stretch beyond where you are today, your Power Talk still needs to be realistic. It shouldn't place extra pressure on you. Nor should it be so unbelievable or improbable that your mind can't effectively use it. For example, it shouldn't be "I am such a great high jumper that I can clear the bar at eight feet with ease." It could be "I am a great high jumper, and eight feet is within my reach."

Troy Tanner, the All-American volleyball player and an Olympic gold medal winner, worked with me at a time when he was having some self-doubts. With my help he created multiple Power Talk statements that reinforced his success and his ability to perform at peak levels. He used these statements to remind himself of what he was capable of doing. One of them was "I reach high, follow through, and rip the ball." When he said it, he *felt* it, and he could see what the hit looked like. At one point Troy asked me, "But what if I'm not actually doing that?" I answered, "You're giving your mind a track to follow."

Troy created another Power Talk statement after we had a conversation in which I told him, "At times in life, people are like velvet, and at other times, they're like steel. Both are appropriate ways to be. The problem is that people sometimes carry that velvet into areas of life where they need to be like steel." Troy realized he had been a little too passive, and so he devised a Power Talk statement that simply said, "I am like steel; bring it on!" Whenever he was on the court, he saw himself as unconquerable, never doubting himself, never cracking, and with an attitude that said "Bring it on!"

Use and repeat your own Power Talk statement every morning and night, and particularly during competition. If you repeat it just before going to sleep, that's a time when your brain is particularly receptive. Power Talk is a way of affirming that you can perform at the level of your statement. Remember, everything is created in the mind first, and Power Talk can help link your mind to your body. *Feel* what you say during Power Talk, especially during competition. If your Power Talk is personal, positive, emotional, and in the present, it is a way to support the athletic outcome that you're seeking.

seven

The Power of Concentration

Bart Starr was one of my first childhood heroes. When I was twelve years old I read a book about his life in which he described how he had developed his passing accuracy and his concentration. He had tied a rope to an old tire, hung it from a tree, and thrown a football through it, thousands of times. He eventually became one of the greatest passers in NFL history.

I figured that if it worked for Bart Starr, it would work for me. So I found an old tire in a nearby industrial park, strung it to a tree, and began throwing the football at it, just like Bart Starr—well, not quite like Bart Starr. No matter how many balls I threw at the target, I just didn't improve very much. No wonder I decided to become a linebacker!

Years later I had a fifteen-minute private conversation with Starr—a truly exciting moment for me. He is a great storyteller, and has related the story of Max McGee, the great tight end with the Green Bay Packers. In one particular game, Starr threw him a perfect pass into the end zone—right into McGee's hands—which he dropped. Later in the same game Starr tossed another pass toward McGee, but this one was an absolutely terrible throw, so bad that McGee had to lunge and twist like an acrobat, straining for the ball—and he caught it. After the game reporters asked McGee how he could drop the perfect pass but somehow pull down the pass that appeared uncatchable. McGee smiled, positioned his hands as if to catch a flawless pass, and said, "You've got to remember, with Bart Starr as my quarterback, I never get to practice catching these."

Of course McGee was joking. Few quarterbacks who ever played the game could put the ball on the money better than Starr. But the extremes of those two passes to McGee illustrate the value of concentration. How often have you "messed up" in a situation that should have been child's play? Nearly everyone has had experiences like this, which occur because we have too much time to think. That's right. The mind gets in the way of our making an easy play. Or we just become too nonchalant because we expect to make the catch. By contrast, when the play is difficult and requires a spontaneous reaction—like Starr's errant pass to McGee—instinct takes over and our bodies do what they need to do.

What can help you focus better and allow your body to perform just the way it knows how to do? I teach my athlete-clients a technique called Concentration Conditioning. It's one that many great athletes have used. Billie Jean King, the pioneering women's tennis player, found this approach especially useful. She would set a tennis ball in front of her and focus on every detail of its surface. She paid close attention to the texture of the yellow covering. She studied all of its seams. She saw everything about it so clearly that when she looked away she could still picture it in her mind's eye in explicit detail.

"Pistol Pete" Maravich, whose basketball skills propelled him into the Hall of Fame in his sport, knew every inch of the basketball, but he also took every opportunity to get to know it even better. As a kid he would blindfold himself and dribble the ball through the house. His concentration was so keen that he could even dribble the basketball outside the car window as his father drove. At the end of each day, when his mother would come in to kiss him good night, she would find him lying in bed, tossing the ball toward the ceiling and catching it. In his book, *Heir to a Dream,* he wrote, "As Mom said good night, she would tuck the ball under my arm, as some mothers would a child's teddy bear, then turn out the light."

I teach football wide receivers to become familiar with everything about the football—how the seams are stitched . . . how the lacing is tied . . . the number of pebbles on the grain . . . where the inflation valve is. It may seem extreme, but it's all part of getting to know their equipment—and ultimately it helps their concentration. During practices and game situations, I instruct receivers to focus their eyes on the tip of the football as it spirals toward them. By concentrating on one spot they're able to avoid any distraction.

▪ CONCENTRATION CONDITIONING ▪

How can you improve your concentration? Imagine that you're a camera, and that your eyes are its lens. Now, pick up the equipment that you use in your sport—whether it's a bowling ball, a hockey puck or stick, or a baseball bat or ball—and stare intently at it. Take an imaginary photograph of every detail. Then turn away. Blink your eyes a couple of times. Next, with your eyes open or closed—preferably open, since you play your sport that way (I hope)—picture on your mind's screen all of the details that you saw when you were actually looking at the object.

If you have difficulty re-creating a clear image, turn to the object again and stare at it intently for about thirty seconds. As you do, say to yourself, "I visualize clearly." Then close your eyes and hold on to that image in your mind's eye for about thirty to forty-five seconds.

Next, blink your eyes twice and then keep them open. Go to the playing field and concentrate on the movements of your sport for a few minutes. How does the football spiral as it leaves your throwing hand? How does a pitched ball curve as it leaves your hand and heads for the outside corner of home plate? How does the dart sail as it heads for the bull's-eye? Then close your eyes and re-create those images in your mind. Concentrate. Study and analyze these movements *now*, before the game itself. As you do, you'll imprint them in your mind, just the way you want them to play out when you're actually performing.

Avoiding distractions is crucial during competition. In a tennis tournament in 1994, Lisa Raymond won the first set (6–4) from Steffi Graf and was leading the second (4–3). But she ultimately lost the match, and afterward explained why. "My mind started to get ahead of me and that was a mistake," she said. "I started thinking, 'Wow, I'm beating the number-one player in the world!' "

As you refine your concentration skills, you need to deal more and more effectively with distractions in the heat of battle. Darrell Pace, who won two Olympic gold medals in archery, has described how he practiced shooting arrows at targets under the noisiest and most disruptive circumstances imaginable. For example, he would set up a makeshift target range next to railroad tracks, or adjacent to a busy road where cars were speeding by. "I had to learn to block everything out," he said.

If you find yourself becoming distracted during competition, quickly remind yourself that you have the power to keep the external commotion from bothering you. You can't control everything that goes on in a football game, for example; but if you stay entirely focused on the tip of the football as it sails toward you, you can completely block out the presence of the defensive back charging toward you, or the crowd noise that's almost deafening. Tony Jacklin, the British golfer, used the term "cocoon of concentration" to describe his mental state when he was on the golf course. During competition, "I'm living *fully* in the present, not moving out of it," Jacklin told the *Sunday Times*. "I'm aware of every half inch of my swing." Dan Fouts, former quarterback for the San Diego Chargers, once said that his ability to concentrate during games was so intense that it was almost like being comatose.

Breathing Your Way to Success

Distractions can take many forms in athletics. You might become rattled by the viciousness of the "trash talk" of an opponent. Or if you've fallen behind in a match that everyone expected you to win, you might find yourself starting to panic, even hyperventilating as you lose your focus on the next point or the next pitch, wondering how you can pull yourself back together.

In a situation like this, one of the quickest ways to get on track is to gain control of your breathing. It sounds pretty simple, doesn't it? After all, from the moment of birth, we've all been breathing—about 26,000 times a day for the average adult—almost always without paying any attention to it. But just think what a crucial, nurturing process breathing is. You can live for thirty days without food, and many days without water. But you can live only about six minutes without a breath of air. Breathing delivers the oxygen that revitalizes all of the cells in the body, including the brain cells that allow clear thinking. It also permits our blood to energize the muscles for strength and endurance.

Just how important is proper breathing? Ask a weight lifter about the role of breathing in his sport. If he's ever tried lifting while inhaling—or after taking just a partial breath—he'll tell you how difficult it is. Breathing affects his performance in many ways, including his ability to muster all his strength, to relax, and to concentrate on the task at hand.

Most people breathe improperly, and not only during sports. They tend to breathe high in their chest, and take shallow, choppy breaths. That creates a buildup of carbon dioxide in their bloodstream, slowing their body's recovery when active and leaving them prone to dizziness and lightheadedness. In the process, this can impair their physical coordination and mental concentration. At times they may begin breathing so rapidly that they find themselves unable to speak.

Take a few moments to pay attention to your own breathing right now. Lightly place one hand on your upper chest and the other hand lightly on your belly. Breathe normally.

Where did you feel the greatest movement? In your chest, or in your belly? Most people breathe primarily with their upper chest; they're called "thoracic breathers." Stress often causes them to breathe this way due to tension and the tightening of the lungs, thus restricting the flow of air. If you're an athlete, that's the *wrong* way to breathe. You need to breathe deep in the belly—what's called "diaphragmatic" or "belly breathing" (the diaphragm is a thin membrane separating the abdominal area and the lungs). You should be taking *deep* breaths, filling up your entire lungs, beginning with the lowest areas and working your way up; when you make use of the lungs in their entirety, you oxygenate the blood more thoroughly than if you rely solely on upper-lung breathing. This method takes practice, but once you perfect it, it is a path toward relaxation and focused attention.

What does diaphragmatic breathing look like? Just watch a baby sleeping. He breathes deeply and rhythmically from the belly. Or observe a lion hunting on *National Geographic*, stalking its prey and then lunging from the bushes to attack an antelope; even under the stress of hunting the lion breathes deeply and rhythmically from the belly (it's not thinking, "Gee, what if I miss the antelope this time?!").

You need to become more like a lion! To perform at peak capacity, take control of your mind and body. Deep, full, relaxed and balanced diaphragmatic breathing lets go of stress and anxiety, steadies the nerves, calms the emotions, and allows you to keep your attention on the next pitch, the next pass, or the next kick on goal.

▪ BELLY BREATHING ▪

Here is a simple breathing exercise to show you just how powerful proper breathing can be:

> Place one hand lightly on your upper chest and the other hand on your belly. Gently take a breath through your nose, inhaling air deep into your lower lungs. Allow your belly to expand without effort as you gradually fill the upper sections of your lung cavity as well. Make sure only the hand on your belly moves; do not move your chest. Hold the breath for two to three seconds.
>
> Next, slowly exhale through your nose. . . . Feel your belly contract as you do. Expel all of the air. Take a little longer to exhale than you did to inhale.
>
> Continue to breathe slowly. With each breath, your belly should rise as you inhale and contract as you exhale. Do this for at least five to seven additional breaths. Feel yourself experience more and more relaxation with each breath.

In the martial arts, one of the first techniques that people learn is to control their breathing—to synchronize the mind (both the left and right hemispheres) with the body so that they become one with what they're trying to accomplish. Yogis learn mind control, and through proper breathing, can do amazing feats (for example, one yogi spent ten hours in a locked box by reducing his oxygen needs to only 30 percent of normal!). And in a sport with ballistic action—like basketball or singles tennis, for example—where rapid recovery is absolutely essential, breathing—and its ability to oxygenate blood quickly—is extremely important.

An Olympic swimmer I worked with had a tendency to become unnerved just before a race. He'd ponder how tough the competition was. He'd worry about what he'd do if he lost. Thinking about everything but the mechanics of the race before him, he would begin to experience butterflies in his stomach and even start hyperventilating as he was about to step onto the starting platform. His left side would actually become numb, almost as if he were paralyzed. But then he learned to take one rhythmic breath after another. As he did, he was able to control his breathing, and when that happened, he could relax quickly and stay focused on the race. Anxiety during competition almost always causes thoracic breathing, but as this swimmer discovered, there are ways to combat it.

Once you learn to breathe properly, you then need to use it in appropriate ways—specifically, for focus and recovery. Not long ago I worked with a baseball player who had learned diaphragmatic breathing very quickly, but applied it at the wrong times. He thought he could incorporate what he had learned throughout the game, from beginning to end—even while he was running at full speed, trying to stretch a single into a double. What he didn't realize was that in those moments of maximum exertion, you just breathe, baby. Afterward, when you need to recover and regain your concentration, that's when you move back into diaphragmatic breathing. Between pitches, when you want to keep calm and relaxed, use this breathing technique. Call upon it at the free-throw line just before you shoot, but not when you're sprinting down the court to dunk the basketball.

Breathing high and shallow actually causes more tension. But rhythmic, diaphragmatic breathing can help you maximize your athletic potential.

Time for Instant Relaxation

Haven't there been moments when you could feel the tension in your body and longed for a way to relax *instantaneously*? Well, there is a way to do it, using a variation of the breathing technique you've just learned. Once you've mastered this Instant Relaxation, you'll be able to enter a relaxed state in just seconds. It adds what I call a "belly blowout" to proper breathing. It begins like the breathing technique above, but then it incorporates some changes.

Before you try this exercise, choose a word that will serve as a Performance Cue to instantly induce relaxation. For some people it might simply be the word "relax," recited gently but firmly. For others it could be "love," "ocean," or "calm." Choose a word that supports a feeling of relaxation, and associate it with a place where you are always content (for me that's on top of a mountain in Yosemite National Park, or on a surfboard out past the breaking waves).

▪ INSTANT RELAXATION ▪

Gently take a slow and effortless breath through your nose, inhaling air deep into your lower lungs. Allow your belly to fully expand as you gradually fill up the upper sections of your lung cavity. Make sure only your belly moves; do not move your chest. Hold the breath for five full seconds.

Next, exhale rapidly, with an initial burst of air that gradually slows as air is expelled fully from the lungs. . . . Now breathe normally again. Enjoy a couple of soothing breaths. . . .

Then take another belly breath. As you do, make a fist with your right hand. . . . Hold both the breath and your fist for about three seconds. . . .

Next, release the air and at the same time open your fist slowly. . . . Allow all tension and anxiety to leave your body. . . .

Now, as you look down at your relaxed, limp right hand, picture your relaxation word in the palm of your hand. . . . When you're feeling completely relaxed, say your cue word aloud while simultaneously squeezing the thumb and forefinger of your hand together firmly yet gently for about one second.

Finally, fully experience all of the sensations of relaxation that you've achieved through this exercise. Spend a few moments enjoying the sensations. . . .

How did you do? Some people think that if they just take a single deep breath, that's all they need to do to relax. But, in fact, a single "sigh" breath may instill even *more* tension in them because in their minds there is a conditioned "woe is me" message that accompanies it. However, the type of diaphragmatic breathing that I've described, along with the physical cues and verbal anchors, will give you a more powerful experience and make relaxation happen much more rapidly. As it does, your heart rate will slow, your muscles will relax, and your breathing will become calmer. Just as important, when you use it during a game, it will clear your mind and let you turn your full attention to the competition at hand.

Practice this Instant Relaxation technique three more times. For most people that's all it takes to learn it. Then, when you want to relax quickly—like during competition—all you'll have to do is say your anchor word while simultaneously squeezing your thumb and forefinger. As you do this you should be able to trigger all of the sensations of relaxation.

Change Your Posture, Change Your Game

When Walter Payton, the great Chicago Bears running back, was breaking rushing records in the NFL, defensive linemen and backs keyed on him. After gaining 5, 10, 20 or more yards per carry, he'd often be smothered by tacklers. But as the players would unpile, Payton was often the first one on his feet, almost jogging back to the huddle. He wanted his opponents to see that no matter how hard they hit him, they couldn't hurt him. The message: "Watch out, because I'm ready to run through you again on the next play."

Your physical posture is not only one of the quickest ways to influence what your opponents think about you, it can change how you feel about yourself as well. It sounds too simple to be true, but your own body posture is a direct link to the brain, and it communicates signals that affect and influence the mind. How you stand and how you present yourself can almost instantly transform your own self-confidence and alter the way others respond to you.

Karch Kiraly is a calm, easygoing guy. But when he plays beach volleyball he elevates his intensity several notches, and never loses sight of just how important his posture is. The air temperature might be 100 degrees, with the sand at 120 degrees, but while his opponents might be clinging to their last gasps of energy, Kiraly's game face and his posture never waver. When the players on the other side of the net have called a time out and are seeking shelter and cold water under the shade of an umbrella, Kiraly has been known to remain in the hot sun, with his hands on his knees, staring straight ahead. To me it's almost a nonhuman response. But the message to his opponents is: "I'm tougher than you, and I'm going to win."

Randy Johnson, who intimidates batters with his 6'10" stature and a wild appearance capped by his long, unkempt hair and goatee, realizes that his presence on the mound is as important as his 95-mile-per-hour fastball. If he trimmed his hair it might be like Sampson cutting off his locks, or Popeye tossing out his spinach. Johnson's "madman" appearance is a powerful contributor to his success. At the same time, it also sends a message to Johnson himself that says, "I'm bad. I'm tough. I'm awesome. No one can get a hit off me."

In the same way, your own posture communicates messages to your psyche. At the University of California at San Francisco, researchers studied people with mild to moderate depression, and noted that they assumed a particular posture. They kept their heads down. They slumped their shoulders. Their breathing was high and shallow. Their facial expression was somewhat contorted, and they looked distressed and disappointed. By contrast, people who were happy instinctively kept their heads up, their shoulders back, had a pleasant look on their faces, and breathed deeply and rhythmically.

The UCSF researchers instructed their depressed patients to make some simple changes in their posture. They had them thrust their shoulders back, lift their chins, keep their eyes focused ahead of them, put a smile on their faces, and deepen their breathing. They instructed them to make a conscious effort to maintain these changes throughout the next few days.

What do you think happened? Much of the depression lifted. The simple act of shifting their posture had sent a signal that the brain responded to immediately. Like a thermostat whose temperature dial has been changed, the brain didn't question it—it just performed.

If you're a man and you start walking like Clint Eastwood or Sylvester Stallone, what happens to your thinking? If you're a woman and you begin carrying yourself like Sharon Stone or Meryl Streep, do you think any differently? Changing your posture *can* make a difference.

▪ POSTURE PERFECT ▪

Try this exercise, which will show you just how powerfully your posture can affect you:

> Step back from your everyday existence and allow some self-defeating thoughts to envelop you. "Life is terrible! . . . Nothing is going right! . . . I'm a loser!" Let these messages sink in. As they do, allow your posture to respond to them. Experience a slumping of your shoulders . . . a drooping of your facial expression . . . a change in your breathing. Notice the ways in which your mental outlook has affected your physical being.
>
> Now, let's make some changes. Lift your head and direct your eyes straight in front of you . . . put a grin on your face . . . pull your shoulders back . . . begin breathing deep and rhythmically . . . clap your hands together three times . . . pump your fist in the air . . . and say aloud, "Yes, I will!"
>
> Next, get in touch with your thoughts. As the brain receives feedback from the body, has your thinking changed? With the shift in posture, haven't you almost instantly taken on a new persona in both mind and body?

Because the brain needs thirty times more blood than other organs, you can't afford to have any interference with this blood flow. We know that posture can affect circulation to the brain, so when your posture is askew—when your shoulders are hunched and there are kinks in your neck—you may be putting pressure on the major arteries that lead to the brain. The result? Inadequate blood supply, fuzzy thinking, forgetfulness, and sometimes strokelike symptoms.

Studies at UCSF and in Europe concluded that even subtle posture changes—including facial expressions—affect emotions and performance. Researchers pinpointed eighteen anatomically different kinds of smiles, each one sending its own distinct message to the brain. There is the hilarious smile, the nervous smile, the flirting smile, and so on. All of them trigger the pathways between body and brain and create real, measurable responses.

Next time you're at a sporting event, watch the posture of the two teams. If you look carefully, the winners and the losers will probably have very different appearances. The posture of the losing team members may convey the message "We just lost; we gave up the big touchdown (basket, run, hit)." However, whether you're winning or losing, it's worth it to cultivate that winning posture.

If you control your posture you can influence your performance. As pitcher Randy Johnson has discovered, looking the part is half the battle.

Becoming the Great Pretender

When I discussed the Ten Perception Stretchers (page 55), I briefly described telling my daughter, a high school volleyball player, that to improve her own game she should act like a college player whom she admired.

That approach really can work. I call it the Great Pretender.

With this exercise you will consciously duplicate the posture, mannerisms, and thoughts of the athlete you most admire. It can help you perform better, and make rapid improvements in your own game.

The Great Pretender is actually something all of us did as children, but generally stopped doing as we became adults. It involves watching others and then patterning ourselves after them—adopting their actions, their behaviors, and even their perceived thoughts.

▪ THE GREAT PRETENDER ▪

Take a moment now to think of an athlete who plays your sport, and one whom you respect and admire. As you think about this individual, concentrate on how she performs. Specifically, notice the expression on her face, her body posture, and the attitude and aura she carries onto the playing field. Study this athlete carefully the next time you see her, either in person or on television.

Next, imagine yourself taking on those characteristics that you've identified with this athlete. In a state of relaxation, and with your eyes closed, picture yourself assuming a facial expression like hers. Also, how would you hold your head? What position would your shoulders be in? What would your breathing be like? What would you be thinking?

Not long ago I worked with a golfer who really admired Fred Couples. However, he had never thought about acting like Couples when he golfed. He told me, "I just figured, 'Well, I'm forty-eight years old, this is the way I am, and I'm never going to get much better.' " I had him try the Great Pretender. That weekend he studied Couples during a televised golf tournament. Then, the next time he was on the course himself, he tried to duplicate what he had seen his role model do. At the tee, he evaluated the fairway in front of him just like Couples did. He approached the ball in the same way, taking a few moments to focus intently on it. He adopted an air of self-confidence that he believed Couples would have. For each of those eighteen holes, in every aspect of his game, he played like Fred Couples. And his score was the best he had achieved in years. "I had a lot more fun, too," he told me.

In giving instructions to a volleyball player, I might say, "Study the player you admire most. Notice how he walks into the gym. Pay attention to what he does just before he first steps onto the court. Evaluate his posture, how he stands, how he positions himself while waiting to serve. Notice how he carries himself, how he prepares for a serve headed his way, how he reacts to a ball being set up for him, and how he responds after winning a point."

Then I'd advise the player, "The next time you're on the court, duplicate what you've seen. Adopt his posture—the same stance, mannerisms, facial expression, and attitude." Immediately this player should find himself playing better. It is one of the quickest ways to change performance.

When I was a boy, *I* was Oscar Robertson. *I* was Jerry West. *I* was Mickey Mantle. *I* was Roberto Clemente. I became whomever I wanted to be, because I wasn't afraid to pretend. And I learned faster by mimicking. You should do the same thing. Duplicate the performance of the athletes you admire and see how far it takes you. I think you'll be pleasantly surprised.

eight

Moving Closer to Peak Performance

Let's begin this chapter with an exercise. One of the most powerful techniques you've learned thus far is the use of Performance Cues to instantly put you in a position to perform at your peak. In the following exercise we'll build on that technique with the Circle of Excellence. As we did earlier, we'll set up "anchors" that, in only a moment, allow you to recall and relive your successes from the past. But as you'll see, you'll take the experience to another level—creating a circle that becomes a Cocoon of Concentration and blocks out all distractions.

THE CIRCLE OF EXCELLENCE

To start, sit in a comfortable chair, close your eyes, and allow yourself to enter a state of relaxation for a minute or two. Then proceed in the following way:

In your mind, go back to a time when you were younger . . . perhaps years ago, or a month ago, or even just a few days ago. Focus on an experience you had that made you feel really good about yourself and your ability to succeed. It may have occurred in sports, or while you were in school or in the work world. Get deeply in touch with this personal achievement, and visualize it and how it made you feel at that time.

As you relive this event from your past, notice how your imagery is much clearer than ever before. You're able to relive experiences like this more vividly than you did when you first used visualization. Immerse yourself totally, embellishing and enjoying the sights, sounds, tastes, smells, tactile sensations, and emotions of that moment. . . .

Next, go back to another time when you were younger still, and you performed the way you wanted to and felt really good about it. Reexperience it as though it were happening now—the expression on your face, the thoughts you were thinking, the confidence that was building within. Enjoy the sounds, sights, tastes, and smells—all the sensations of that time—as the images become more intense and more exciting. . . . As you relive that moment, notice how good it makes you feel. . . .

Then think of a third experience, this time even farther back in your past, another experience that made you feel good about what you had accomplished. Perhaps it was something that you weren't sure you could do, but you excelled in it anyway. As you recall it, feel every emotion, see every sight, and hear every sound that was part of it. Relish the moment all over again, and as you do, tell yourself, "This is fantastic." . . .

Next, choose a Performance Cue to give permanence to these experiences. It could be a word like "Excellent" or "Great." Try limiting it to one

word and one word only. It will become a cue that
you associate so firmly with the successes in your
past, that when you say it in the heat of battle it
will instantly trigger only positive emotions and
experiences.

Now, notice an imaginary circle in front of
you. It is your Circle of Excellence. Take a moment
to look closely at it. . . . What color is your circle?
Is it elevated above ground level, so you need to
step up to get into it? Within the circle, is there a
platform that resembles an Olympic victory
stand? . . . In your mind's eye create a clear, vivid
picture of your own circle.

This circle is unique to you, and it will intensify the feelings of past successes and remind your
body that it can succeed. When you step into it in
a few moments, your past successes will become
even more powerful. This circle will become a Cocoon of Concentration, and will instantly fire up
all the memories in your brain that cause your
body to perform better and that stimulate the
Maximum Athletic Performance State in an instant. It will turn up the volume and make everything about those experiences more powerful.

Now it's time. In your imagination, step into
your Circle of Excellence. As you do, simultaneously say your cue word or anchor aloud, with
passion and belief. . . . At that moment, allow all
the feelings about those past successes to intensify.
Everything in your mind's eye will become more
positive and success-oriented. As your images and
feelings reach a peak, put them into your right

hand (or, if you're left-handed, into the left) and squeeze your fist tightly three times as you say your cue word. Feel the emotions completely envelop you, and as that happens, acknowledge that they enhance your ability to succeed. . . .

Finally, step out of the Circle of Excellence. Recognize that in the midst of competition, you can reenter the circle and, with the help of your cue word, relive these same feelings of success in an instant.

Not long ago I taught the Circle of Excellence exercise to a wide receiver who had been out of football for a while and thought his opportunity to play professionally was over. But by learning to enter the circle and using this extra boost of self-confidence just before a recent tryout, he caught the ball better than ever before. Today he is playing in the NFL.

In an instant, you can use the Circle of Excellence to set aside any nervousness or anxieties you have before or during a game and replace them with the self-confidence you need to stay cool and confident in the heat of battle. You'll fully expect to achieve your athletic goals—and you will.

How Prepared Are You?

A golfer is competing in a tournament that she considers crucial to her career. She's playing a great round, and is within reach of winning the tournament. However, on the eighteenth hole, she tees off and slices the ball into the rough. As she approaches the ball where it landed, she is stunned to see that it has rolled into a paper bag that a spectator has left behind. The tournament officials won't let her remove the ball from the bag unless she's willing to take a penalty. She ponders her dilemma, and then comes up with an idea. She requests a cigarette lighter from her caddy, bends down, and sets fire to the bag. After it burns to ashes, she approaches the ball with a three-iron and takes her shot without a penalty.

This golfer took a few moments to think through her situation, and she came up with a workable solution. This process, called "prethought," is a key to winning with the Mental Edge. It's a way to maximize your performance by using your brain before you use your brawn. You prepare yourself by thinking about what's ahead and doing everything possible to give it all you've got.

"Be prepared" is more than the Boy Scout motto. If you are fully ready, both mentally and physically, before the opening kickoff or the first jump ball, you have a much greater chance of excelling—and thoroughly enjoying the process of competition.

When Fran Tarkenton was leading the Minnesota Vikings to victories and Super Bowls, sports journalist Eliot Asinof wrote that the great quarterback would think of almost nothing other than the opposing team that he'd face on the following Sunday. Visualization exercises were an important part of his preparation, and he would become so immersed in those images that he felt as though he were walking around on another planet. In his mind's eye he would review every player on the defensive team, picturing their moves, their speed, their strengths, their weaknesses, the sounds of their footsteps as they would chase him out of the pocket, and how he would escape their charge. He would run entire plays in his head, down to the tiniest details. By Sunday afternoon he was fully prepared.

Tarkenton told Asinof, "I'm trying to visualize every game situation, every defense they're going to throw at me. I tell myself, 'What will I do on their five-yard line and it's third and goal to go, and our short passing game hasn't been going too well and their line looks like a wall and we're six points behind?' " Because of his preparation, Tarkenton knew exactly what the Vikings offense was going to do in every conceivable situation that might arise. No wonder he was a winner.

Greg Lemond was another stellar athlete for whom prethought often meant the difference between winning and finishing second. In the 1989 Tour de France bicycle race, he seemed like the unlikeliest of winners. With only the final 27-kilometer (15.2 miles) leg of the 2,023-mile event remaining, Lemond was fifty seconds behind Frenchman Laurent Fignon—a gap considered insurmountable in a sport in which gaining just a single second per kilometer is considered virtually impossible.

But Lemond had overcome huge obstacles before. In fact, just two years earlier he had nearly died in a hunting accident that shattered two ribs, collapsed a lung, perforated vital organs (including the liver, kidney, and intestines), and left more than thirty lead shotgun pellets in his body. To Lemond, something as "simple" as making up fifty seconds seemed within reach, even if no one else believed it was possible.

In prethought, Lemond created a winning strategy. He knew that the physical differences between him and

Fignon were negligible; both of their bodies were finely tuned machines. But Lemond believed that he could gain an edge by outthinking his competitor. After twenty-three days of racing, the last thing he could accept was to lose the race by just a few seconds. "I wanted this so badly that I was willing to pedal until I burst," he said. He mentally plotted a strategy that would give him an advantage in the final kilometers of the race. He decided that riding a different style of bicycle in the last leg would make a difference, and so he switched bicycles. He wore an aerodynamic helmet different from any of those worn by the other cyclists. He adopted a mind-set to achieve the impossible, while Fignon was just trying to "hang on."

Lemond felt fully prepared when the final day dawned. And, in fact, he worked a miracle on the course. His average speed on that last sprint from Versailles to Paris was 34 miles per hour—the fastest ever for a single day in the event. He steadily closed the gap between himself and Fignon, and finally passed him. He crossed the finish line eight seconds ahead of his competitor—the narrowest victory margin in the race's history.

Like Fran Tarkenton and Greg Lemond, you need to know everything that lies ahead and plan for every contingency. When I give seminars, I check the room, the seating, the microphone, and the slide projector in the hours before I take the stage. I don't want any surprises. Many times that kind of prethought has saved me a lot of irritation. You need to have complete familiarity with the tools and equipment you are going to use—including your mind and body.

Let me give you another example of the value of knowing your equipment. When John Havlicek, the NBA

Hall of Famer, was warming up for a game with the Boston Celtics, he sensed something wrong with one of the baskets. He approached a referee just minutes before tipoff and said, "The hoop is off by two inches!" The referee looked at him in disbelief, and probably would have ignored Havlicek's concerns if the basketball great hadn't been so persistent. The referee finally measured the basket, and sure enough, it was two inches from its regulation height! Prethought involves knowing what you're up against—and then preparing fully for what's ahead.

Keeping the Joy in Athletics

Okay, let's say you've done all the necessary preparation before game time. You're now ready to take the field—a time when you need to leave all of your analysis (and, in many instances, *over*analysis) in the locker room. Remember, once the competition begins, too much analysis can sabotage your performance, as well as take the fun out of it. Use techniques like Performance Cues (page 108) and Power Talk (page 113) for an instant shot in the arm during the game itself. But after the starting gun has fired, let your body take over and do what your physical and mental training programs have prepared it to do.

Whether you're smashing racquetballs off the front wall, spinning curveballs toward home plate, or nailing triple axels on the ice, you should thoroughly enjoy the process while you're doing it. Once you're in the heat of competition you should find the experience gratifying (otherwise, why do it?). If you've prepared properly, getting results will take care of itself.

Part of that preparation, of course, is working out before you compete. Too often, in conversations with both amateur and professional athletes, they tell me that their workouts seem like "punishment" (after all, they are called *work*outs!). If you've been told by your doctor, for example, to walk forty-five minutes a day to keep your heart healthy, you may think of it as drudgery and as something you *have* to do. Even many elite athletes, when they're pushing themselves to the limit and experiencing both physical and emotional pain, haven't been able to find the pleasure in exercise at that moment.

Part of the problem rests with one's mind-set. When you decide that training is necessary to turn you into a winner or a champion, then the process becomes more enjoyable as you keep the goal in the forefront of your mind. One athlete told me, "When I recognized that training was a privilege, and that it allowed me to keep my body fit, then it became fun." Another said, "My athletic talents are a gift from God, and the way I use my talents shows my appreciation for this gift."

Think back to when you were a child. You couldn't wait to go outdoors to *play*. You raced to the park because you loved running and jumping—not because you were struggling to be the best runner and jumper in the city, or were driven to set a world's record. It was fun—and it still can be.

To keep your workouts positive you need to avoid overtraining and burnout. Make sure you schedule some time away from your workouts now and then—even a day off every week can give you a breather. The body needs a chance to recover, and so does the mind. A break here and there can momentarily silence your mind and recharge those batteries in both the brain and body.

Moving Past the Pain

There is a downside to overtraining that I haven't discussed yet. Piling it on makes you more vulnerable to injuries, which can undermine your mental and physical training programs faster than you can say "torn Achilles tendon." Injuries can keep you on the sidelines, sabotaging all of your efforts toward peak performance.

But even though you can minimize your risk of injuries, they can still happen from time to time. Terms like "runner's knee" and "tennis elbow" have become part of everyone's vocabularies and keep thousands of us reaching frequently for ice packs and bottles of aspirin or ibuprofen. When injuries do occur, you can also fight back with the Mental Edge.

In recent years I've worked with a volleyball player named Liz Masakayn, who had undergone reconstructive surgery on her knee and made a remarkable comeback. But one afternoon after she had returned to the court she jumped to drill the ball across the net, landed awkwardly on that knee, and her kneecap shattered. Doctors told her that she'd probably never play again, and even if she did, she'd never be able to play the same type of game.

Not surprisingly, Liz was devastated as much by the prognosis as the injury. She had to confront a future that might not have any volleyball in it, or in the best-case scenario, she'd have to abandon the aggressive power game that she loved playing. There was a part of her, however, that refused to accept the doctor's verdict completely. So when she was able, she launched into a different type of training program designed to rehabilitate her knee fully— and to mentally prepare her to return to the dynamic style of competing that had been a part of her game and her life for years.

Liz did make it back—all the way back. She had stuck to her plan for complete healing. Then she won a major tournament in her first year after returning to the circuit. She made it onto the victory platform, despite her doctor's ominous predictions.

Many athletes are ruined after suffering major injuries. They're never the same players they once were, becoming tentative and playing their sport differently than they had before. They become "psyched out" and afraid of reinjury. But there are ways to return to your top form—and beyond. Many of the exercises I've already described in this book can help (Liz used to visualize herself on the victory platform at volleyball tournaments). But as much as anything, the athletes I've seen recover fully from their injuries have been driven by a determination that says, "You're not going to stop me." They stay focused on their athletic goals, renew their commitment to them every day, and adopt the belief "Others have come back; so can I."

In baseball, for example, a severe rotator cuff injury was once considered a "death sentence" to a pitching career. But Orel Hershiser underwent major reconstructive shoulder surgery and proved that comebacks were possible. Tommy John did the same with a devastating elbow injury, undergoing a pioneering tendon transplantation that breathed new life into his baseball career. More recently, American downhill skier Picabo Street underwent reconstructive knee surgery before the 1998 Winter Olympics—and battled back to win a gold medal in Nagano. Stories like that have inspired many injured athletes of lesser renown to fight the good fight along the road back.

Visualization is one way to facilitate the healing process and get beyond the mental barriers to your recovery. I have had back problems in recent years, and I've consistently activated the Mental Edge to promote healing. I've studied the X rays and MRIs of my injured back and then examined illustrations of a healthy back. These healthy images were the ones I hoped to recapture. I began to picture my back the way I wanted it to be, with the vertebrae perfectly interlocked and the disks free of bulging. I repeatedly visualized my back in a healed, whole condition. Has this helped the healing process? I can't say definitively, but I do know that visualization is sending a signal to my body that appears to promote recovery. It also makes me feel better because I'm not a helpless victim.

Perhaps you're familiar with the work of physicians and other health-care professionals who have used visualization as an adjunct to conventional treatments for a variety of serious diseases, including cancer. They may teach their patients to picture their white blood cells as white knights attacking and destroying their malignancies. Or, when patients describe their back pain as "being on fire," they may teach them visualization exercises in which imaginary clouds release rainwater on those flames, dousing the fire and easing the pain. There is growing evidence that this type of imagery can mobilize the autonomic nervous system and the body's healing immune system.

For this reason I believe it's worth trying visualization to stimulate your recovery from sports-related injuries.

Picture your body in a state of full recovery. Imagine your injury being nourished by a bright light of healing energy capable of returning your body to good health. This might be a way to speed up the process that gets you back onto the playing field.

Meanwhile, during your recovery, you can use imagery in another way. Mentally rehearse your sports performance. This can help you stay as sharp as possible during your layoff from training and competition. Use visualization to picture yourself performing to perfection, making every move in your sport absolutely flawlessly. During the months in which Liz Masakayn could not actually work out, she would visualize her past successes and picture how she was going to perform in the future. It kept her enthusiasm high, and it may have accelerated her successful transition back into actual competition.

When You Hurt . . .

"No pain, no gain." That may be the philosophy of some coaches, but it's not mine. Yes, you do need to experience pain to make progress as an endurance runner or power lifter. But you need to differentiate between the burning of lactic acid in the muscles and the burning of a tendon that's about to snap! In general, I don't believe that pushing yourself to the point of exhaustion or physical pain is going to improve your performance. In fact it's more likely to dampen your enthusiasm for the game, cause injuries, and perhaps lead you to quit altogether.

But when you do become injured—coping with a sprained ankle or a sore throwing arm—there may be times when you *have* to practice and play in pain. An athlete who has trained all her life for the Olympics is going to compete in the Games when she hurts because it's a chance she may never get again. This kind of situation, however, is more the exception than the rule.

As I tell my own client-athletes, "You can't ride a charley horse." Yes, you can play in pain, but you won't play as well. If you hurt, you need to get healthy—and you also need to get smart quickly. In planning a strategy, answer the question, "Is this temporary discomfort, or is it something that can lead to permanent, irreversible injury?" If it's only a bruise or a mild ankle twist, then you can probably "suck it up" safely and play through it. But if it's a slightly torn tendon, for example, you might snap the tendon completely if you try to compete, which would put you on the sidelines for months. You may need to rely on your physician or trainer to help you determine whether an injury is something that requires rest.

If you do decide to play, the mental techniques in this book can help you push that pain into the background, allowing you to concentrate on your performance. You can move into a zone in which your awareness of pain is minimized by disengaging yourself from the sensations of discomfort. Runners of endurance races, for example, often experience pain as they clock one mile after another. But with the Mental Edge, they can distract themselves from the discomfort and concentrate on the race itself or on their surroundings, real or imagined. In a study published in the journal *Cognitive Therapy and Research,* in which joggers exercised on a treadmill, those who focused on the rhythm of their feet landing on the treadmill surface worked out 32 percent longer than volunteers who had not learned to distract themselves this way.

In the days when I competed in triathlons, I was once running the last leg of the event on a summer day in Omaha, when the temperature was 102 degrees and the humidity was pushing 70 percent. We were running on asphalt, there was steam rising from its surface, and the race was becoming a killer. At that point I switched gears mentally. I began picturing myself running in the cool, comfortable weather of Lake Tahoe. The images I created in my mind were so real that I could actually feel the coolness of the mountain air, smell the pine trees, and enjoy the sights of the crystal-blue lake. For much of that race Omaha felt as though it were a million miles away.

Other long-distance runners have distracted themselves by listening to imaginary music as they ran or by doing math problems in their mind. I've also encouraged people to use the Great Pretender (page 133) during times when modest pain is interfering with their performance.

I recently introduced a variation of the Great Pretender to a seventy-year-old golfer who was eager to get back onto the course shortly after having kidney surgery. His first couple rounds of golf weren't much fun. He was experiencing a lot of discomfort that was interfering with his enjoyment of the game. I suggested that he adopt components of the Great Pretender. I asked him questions like, "If you could perform effortlessly, if you had no pain, how would you be standing? . . . If you could drive the ball straight and true, what kind of expression would you have on your face, and how would you be breathing?" He pretended that he was free of pain, and although he wasn't able to eradicate every sensation of discomfort, it became such a minor distraction that he performed much better in his next round. "I've never enjoyed and appreciated golf so much in my life," he told me with a sigh of relief. He became another success story of the Mental Edge.

nine

Going Beyond Normal

Every great achiever—whether in sports, business or any other endeavor—is never content just doing what everyone else does. Every high achiever *goes beyond normal.*

Need some proof? In the field of athletics, look at the men and women who excel. Jerry Rice, for example, has always gone *way* beyond normal. To become one of the greatest pass receivers in NFL history, he has trained harder than just about anyone. His diet has been better and more finely tuned. Mentally he is sharper than the rest. Rice has always believed in himself and has constantly added new elements to every component of his program. When he got good, he wanted to become better; when he got better, he wanted to become great; when he became great, he wanted to be the best in football annals. He has pursued the highest achievements possible, all of the time.

As an athlete, you can go beyond normal without pushing yourself to the brink of burnout. You should work hard toward becoming the best you can be, but without putting undue pressure on yourself. Here's my recommendation: in the weeks and months ahead, evaluate every aspect of your program at least every thirty days, and go the extra mile. Make a commitment to move beyond where you are today and to do more than most of your peers. Here are some important steps in this process:

1. Congratulate yourself on already adopting the Mental Edge program. In the weeks and months ahead it is going to produce enormous improvements in your athletic performance. Keep at it. Work with it regularly. Make it a permanent part of your life.

2. Evaluate what you eat. Are you sticking to a nutritious eating plan, or are you eating like a world-class junk-food junkie? Are you consuming foods from all of the major food groups, or are you stuck on doughnuts and potato chips? You need to find a sound nutritional program that works for you and hang tough with it.

The major reason that people don't follow a sensible eating plan is the mental aspect of it. They feel like they're depriving themselves, and giving up something (can they really live without Twinkies and Big Macs?!). The Mental Edge can help you stick with a healthy, performance-promoting nutritional program. It will change your entire mind-set and move you toward a commitment to a well-rounded dietary plan that will contribute to reaching your athletic goals.

In my consulting work I've seen tremendous variations in the nutritional needs of athletes. I've worked with dietitians and doctors in developing a program in which athletes can adopt an eating plan unique to their own metabolic type and sport. Some athletes need more of their calories from carbohydrates (or protein or fat) than others. The key for you is to work with a nutritionist or a dietitian (your doctor can refer you to one); he or she can create a personalized eating plan that meets your own body's needs. Once you have a program that's right for you, commit to it. (A full description of my own Performance Zone Nutrition plan is beyond the scope of this book about the Mental Edge, but you can learn more about it by calling the 800 number in the back of the book.)

3. Go the extra mile in your physical training. Talk to coaches about the latest breakthroughs in training (there is always something new, like plyometrics, overspeed training, and innovations in weight lifting). Stay up to date. Look for something to keep you ahead of the pack and moving beyond normal.

In chapter 4 I described a high school basketball player I've worked with who has refused to let any obstacle undermine his dream of playing college basketball. He took an inventory of his genetic gifts and realized that he wasn't the fastest or the strongest basketball player, nor was he the highest jumper. He concluded that he had to train differently to excel. So he adopted a program incorporating weight training, jump training, and speed training. He changed the way he ate and incorporated the Mental Edge into his life. Before long he was playing over the top, and dunking the basketball about mid-forearm-high. I believe he'll soon be playing in a Division I college basketball program.

Why don't more athletes go beyond normal in their training? Many won't allow themselves to make the mental quantum leap of letting go of the way they've trained for years. Karch Kiraly is an exception to this common phenomenon. He is in his mid-thirties and his career as a beach volleyball player should probably be over by now. But Karch is always looking for something new and better to incorporate into his training. He is a world-class athlete who has recognized that being like everyone else isn't good enough. He has to go beyond normal.

The Mental Saboteurs of Your Game

Have you ever been in a situation where you felt thoroughly prepared for an athletic competition, but a mental glitch undermined all of those hours of preparation? Maybe you became psyched-out by the trash talking of opponents. Or perhaps you found yourself rattled by playing in front of fans cheering wildly for the other team. Let's look at these issues more closely:

The Trials of Trash Talking

Imagine yourself competing in a crucial football or basketball game, and just minutes into it, an opposing player gets in your face. "Moving a little slow today, buddy?" he says. Instantly your confidence heads south. "Am I really playing slower than usual?" you ask yourself. Before long you're overthinking, overanalyzing, and your intensity and skill levels suffer. Or he may say something disparaging about "yo' mama," and rather than playing basketball, all you want to do is fight.

Trash talking seems like an inevitable fact of life these days, and it can be intimidating. Negative comments and even threats can cause you to lose focus—and lose the game. If you pay too much attention to trash talk and take it to heart, you're going to start playing just like your opponent wants you to.

When trash talk is directed your way, turn it into a positive. Tell yourself, "I'm not slow today. I'm as fast as I've ever been." Or "My mama's the best!" Then keep your concentration on the next play or the next pitch and call upon the techniques of the Mental Edge to stay focused. If you respond or talk back to an opponent, that's exactly what he wants you to do. When that happens, your attention has strayed, your anger may soar, and you're not going to play well.

Keep in mind that, at times, trash talk can be subtle. As you're ready to shoot a free throw you might hear, "Make sure your toes aren't over the line"; or, "Whatever you do, don't shoot it short." Those comments can give you something else to think about and distract you from the shot you're about to take.

Here's another example of the power of subtle trash talk: not long ago I was competing in a two-man beach volleyball tournament sponsored by Bud Light, and the beer company had applied a long strip of tape with the product name on it, extending the full length of the top edge of the net. Knowing the power of negative seeds, I chose a critical point of the match, and shouted to my teammate, "What's your favorite beer?" He responded, "Bud Light!" as we both looked at the tape. That comment planted a seed with our opponents, who promptly served the next ball right into the top of the tape! This technique had worked so well that I used it at opportune moments throughout the tournament, and about 80 percent of the time the serve either hit the tape or went long as our opponents overcompensated to make sure the ball didn't strike the net. The trash talking wasn't demeaning, but it successfully "got into the heads" of the opposition.

What's the bottom line? When you're the target of trash talk—a comment such as "You just can't hit the jumper today!"—turn it around internally at once. Put up a wall that keeps the remark from sinking all the way in and reframe it into something positive. Tell yourself, "I can hit that shot; watch me!" Or, "I have perfect form and follow-through." Take the negative comment and transform it into an internal message that will *raise* the level of your game, not disrupt it.

The Home Field Advantage

Do you play better on your home court or home field, compared to being on the road? Frankly, most athletes do, but it shouldn't be that way.

If you're a high school football player the field on your own campus is exactly the same as the field of your crosstown rival. It's 100 yards long from goal line to goal line. Its width is 160 feet. The crossbar of the goal posts is precisely 10 feet high. The ball is exactly the same—about 11 inches long, 7 inches in diameter at the center, and weighs about 14 to 15 ounces. All the rules of the game—from offsides to clipping to holding—are identical.

The only difference, in fact, may be a mental one. When playing away from home you may *perceive* being at a disadvantage. The crowd is cheering for your opponents,

not for you, and that might unnerve you. But if you're prepared, physically and mentally, you can play just as well
on the road as you do at home.

Consider the Denver Broncos, winners of the Super
Bowl in 1998. The Broncos were a wild card team in the
post-season, meaning that *none* of their playoff games was
in the familiar surroundings of Mile High Stadium. But the
Bronco players knew they were a great team, no matter
where they were competing. They believed they were good
enough to win anywhere. And they did win game after
game, all the way to the Super Bowl.

The Parent Trap

Here is a message for parents: if your children are
playing sports—whether in Little League or at the high
school or college level—you can be their greatest ally, or a
saboteur of their performance. Just like the trash talker
who gets into an athlete's head, you can undermine their
play—or help them perform better—through your behavior, advice, and remarks.

See if this common scenario sounds familiar: a parent
places his child on a pedestal, perceiving him as a super-
star-in-the-making. Maybe the youngster is the quarterback of his Pop Warner football team at age twelve, and
in Dad's eyes, he's already a sure bet to make the NFL
Hall of Fame. Inevitably those kinds of expectations will
get communicated to the boy, either directly or subtly.
And that's a heavy burden for a child to carry. He'll believe that to please his father he has to remain the star of
the team as he moves into high school, but that isn't al-

ways possible. Some of his teammates may catch up to or surpass him in terms of their size and playing ability.

So after years of always being the best, this young athlete may become only "one of the pack." When that happens, he may feel even more pressure, real or imagined, from Dad. At the age of sixteen he may drop out of sports altogether, no longer able to cope with the stress associated with his father's fantasies and finding that sports aren't fun anymore. Not surprisingly, from the ages of fourteen to eighteen, many thousands of boys and girls quit athletics altogether, sometimes rebelling with negative, destructive behavior as they break free from pushy parents and feelings of failure.

You need to let your children develop at their own pace, choose the sports they're going to play, and decide how long they're going to play them. *They've* got to make the decisions. Only then can they fulfill their potential. Support them, offer them opportunities to refine their physical and mental skills, but let it be *their* choice whether to take advantage of those opportunities. *Every* athlete who works with me on the Mental Edge does so because he or she wants to, not because a parent demands it. I make sure of that. It needs to be the young athlete's choice, not the parent's decision.

Stop trying to pressure your children into becoming what *you* want them to be. Show this book to the young athletes in your family, let them read about and develop their own Mental Edge, but don't insist that they follow every twist and turn along the path that you envision for them. It's not fair, and it's not going to work.

Keeping a Winning Attitude

Whether you hope to putt more accurately in your Saturday morning foursomes or you're dreaming of a gold medal at the 2000 Olympic Games in Australia, the Mental Edge program has a lot to offer. By now I think you've recognized that the mental side of sports can give you an important advantage toward achieving whatever your athletic goals are.

To help you develop and maintain a winning attitude, there are six steps I'd like you to keep in mind, now and in the months and years ahead. If you follow these guidelines you will maximize your chances of success:

1. *Let go of your ego.* Accept criticism with good spirit and without taking it personally. Remember that when someone criticizes aspects of your athletic performance, he or she does not usually have a malicious intent. Rather than an attack, it may be meant as something constructive. But even if those comments are petty and poisonous, you don't have to take them personally. Don't make them your problem. Respond by saying, "That's something to think about," and move on.

In some instances you may be able to learn a few things from the criticism—if you're willing to set aside your ego and respond to the comments objectively. Ask yourself, "How can this help me?" Dissociate yourself from any emotional wounds that the comments could inflict, and process the information for the positive elements it may contain. Take what you can learn from it (if anything) and incorporate it into your athletic program.

Remember, your coach might criticize you only because he sees it as a way of helping you improve your game, although if that criticism isn't offered in a constructive way it can be emotionally devastating. Some coaches communicate with athletes only through negative comments, never offering praise. That's a tragedy. Don't give up on sports because you have a coach who has terrible social skills or is simply a jerk. This may be a time when you need to change coaches or teams rather than quitting altogether.

Never allow yourself to become overwhelmed by the negative influence of others. Tough it out. Get a second opinion. Make a concerted effort to surround yourself with people who are positive, who will allow you to reach for your dreams, and who will support you in that effort. Ultimately, let your performance on the playing field speak for itself.

Donnie Moore was a talented relief pitcher with the California Angels, but one game—really, just one pitch— changed his life forever. In the fifth game of the American League championship series in 1986, the Angels led in the ninth inning and were only one strike away from winning their first pennant ever. But Dave Henderson of the Boston Red Sox blasted a Moore pitch over the left field fence for a two-run homer; the Angels lost the game and the championship, and Moore never recovered emotionally. He took the defeat as personally as an athlete could, eventually left baseball—and committed suicide. Yes, this incident is an extreme case, but it can serve as a reminder that sports are something you do; they're not you. Sports aren't a matter of life and death. Don't take things personally. Let go of your ego. Be the best you can be and don't worry about how others view you.

2. *Keep your sense of humor.* Be willing to laugh at yourself. Life really is fun, and so are sports. If you have a particularly disappointing game, find the humor in it. Look for something to laugh about in anything negative that takes place. As one baseball player quipped, "I was very consistent today—consistently bad!"

3. *View change as an opportunity.* Whenever you experience an apparent setback, find a way to reposition yourself and use it to your advantage. Dennis Eckersley was a starting pitcher in the early part of his career, and even became a twenty-game winner. One season, however, his manager moved him to the bullpen, which stunned him. He saw this as a clear demotion. But after the initial shock wore off, he decided to make the most of it—and he really did. Eckersley went on to become the all-time best closer in baseball history. However, he didn't become great until he made up his mind to view that supposed demotion as an opportunity, not as a slap in the face. Today Eckersley is still one of the most feared relief pitchers in the game.

4. *Decide in advance what you want.* Plan ahead as much as possible. How do you want your day to go? What do you need to do today and in the days ahead to move closer to your goals? What's the best way to respond to your coach, teammates, and opponents in various situations? How will you react to victories and defeats when they occur? The more advance planning you do, the better.

5. *Temporary letdowns are normal.* Accept the reality that life and sports have peaks and valleys. Late in his stel-

lar career George Brett clearly learned this fact of life. In his late thirties Brett became one of the oldest baseball batting champions ever. But in the year he won that title, he got off to a terrible start, and performed disappointingly until the All-Star break. But then he caught fire. He really wasn't doing anything differently at the plate; he just kept doing the things that had made him successful in the past. By the time the season ended he had sizzled his way to a batting title.

So don't give up. Work through the setbacks. Grow from them. Learn from them. Make adjustments when necessary. Stay focused on your goals and view the letdowns within the context of striving to fulfill your dreams.

6. *Take some time off.* As I mentioned earlier in this chapter, you need to get away from the training field now and then. Schedule days off regularly. Do something fun, taking your mind off your sport. Perhaps all you need is a breather to see things clearly and begin anew with a fresh outlook.

One of the most inspiring stories I've heard revolves around Colonel James Hall, who was a prisoner of war in North Vietnam for more than five years. He was in isolation, rarely seeing another human being other than the enemy soldiers who brought him food. His only real companion was his very active mind. He had loved to play golf back home, but obviously had no opportunity for that in the POW camp. In his mind, however, he'd picture himself competing in his favorite sport. He'd replay many of his past matches over and over in his mind's eye. He'd smell the grass; he'd feel the breeze across his face. He'd experience the sensations of swinging a driver and of stroking a putt into the cup. In his mind, he'd play a round of golf every day, sometimes at Pebble Beach, other times at Augusta. It was a wonderful distraction from the cruel reality in which he found himself.

When Colonel Hall was finally released from captivity, he got the chance to return to an actual golf course for the first time in years. While playing in a pro-am tournament with pro golfer Orville Moody, Colonel Hall shot his best score ever.

This is an amazing testament to the power of the mind and the amazing benefits of maintaining a positive outlook. You have what it takes to be positive in any circumstance.

ten

The Mental Edge:
Now and in Your Future

Abraham Maslow, the renowned American psychologist and founder of humanistic psychology, once said, "If you deliberately plan to be less than you're capable of being, then I warn you that you'll be deeply unhappy for the rest of your life."

I love that statement. So often athletes at all levels are content just to get through the next practice and the next game, without giving much thought to reaching their full potential. While I don't think any of us have to win gold medals to feel successful, we should feel good about what we're striving for and what we're accomplishing. The Mental Edge can help you do just that.

Attitude Is Everything

No matter what your background, and no matter how many advantages in life you did or didn't have, you *can* maximize the potential that may still be sleeping within you. Walter Payton, the great Chicago Bears running back, faced plenty of obstacles in his path toward football greatness, but he wouldn't take no for an answer. Payton grew up in a small town. His mother was a seamstress, his father was a custodian, and they taught him the value of hard work and the importance of an optimistic attitude. Although they lived in an industrial area on the edge of the city dump, the young Payton made the best of his environment. He used his imagination to thrive in difficult circumstances and to dream of a brighter future.

Payton was of average size and thus was an unlikely candidate to eventually excel in the NFL. But he loved football, and by applying the work ethic he had learned from his parents, he turned himself into a superstar. When Payton lifted weights, his training partners couldn't keep up with him, so he often lifted alone. His running workout was brutal, and included a sprint up a 60-yard hill that looked almost vertical. He'd run until his legs felt like rubber; then he'd walk down the hill and do it again—and again and again.

When Payton began playing for the Bears, they were one of the worst teams in the league. But he never openly complained. He never demanded to be traded. He just ran hard, game after game—breaking tackles, straight-arming opponents, and blasting his way to an NFL rushing title. He never quit, thanks to his winning attitude, and in time his teammates adopted the same attitude. The desire to win became contagious. Eventually, once the Bears got a new coach and some new players, they started winning. During the 1985 season they climaxed an 18–1 season with a Super Bowl victory. Not surprisingly, Payton played incredibly that season. He achieved his third straight 2,000-yard season combining runs and catches. He also rushed for 100 or more yards in nine consecutive games—another NFL record at the time.

Many football aficionados consider Walter Payton to be the best football player, pound for pound, in NFL history. It was his winning attitude that got him, and the Bears, their Super Bowl rings.

Other great athletes have possessed the same strong drive to succeed. Althea Gibson was the first black woman tennis player to compete on center court in Wimbledon. She didn't allow her color to stop her. She let racism slide off her back. She kept her focus on playing tennis. In both 1957 and 1958 she won the Wimbledon championship, capitalizing on an inextinguishable desire to succeed.

As you plot your own athletic future, accept responsibility for what has happened to you thus far and for shaping what will happen in the future. Don't blame life or circumstances; accept the hand you were dealt and make the most of it. Mr. T (of the *Rocky* movies) once said, "I may be from the ghetto, but there's no ghetto in me." Where you come from does not have to be a limit on where you end up. If you activate the mental side of your game, you can soar higher than you might ever have imagined.

Capitalizing on the Power Cycle

To help you get the most out of the Mental Edge, let's spend part of this final chapter briefly reviewing the important steps of the program that I've described in this book. They are the elements of the Six-Step Power Cycle. If you incorporate each of these steps into your training and competition, you'll find yourself making giant strides in improving your athletic performance.

1. Posture. Your posture is a direct link to the brain, and it can dramatically influence your self-confidence and your performance. Assume the body posture you would have if you were playing at peak levels. How would you be standing if you were at the top of your game? How would you be moving? What would your facial expression be? How would you be breathing? Assume and maintain that posture and your game will improve.

2. *Power Talk*. This technique sends messages to the brain and body and builds feelings of success. Power Talk is a way of affirming that you can perform at the next level. You can use it to propel yourself to the highest levels of your potential. Use Power Talk when you practice and compete. Get excited about it. Get passionate about it. Say it with belief.

3. *Visualization*. Use all of your senses to create vivid, three-dimensional images that can prepare you to train and perform. By using your mind to play and replay the precise experiences that you want to have on the athletic field, you can form direct links to the body that increase your likelihood of turning those images into reality.

4. *Success History Search*. Use the Success History Search to recreate vivid pictures of past successes that reestablish old connections between the brain and the body. Embrace those feelings of accomplishment—the sights, sounds, emotions, and thoughts—and allow them to prepare you for future achievements.

5. *Performance Cues*. Choose one or more cue words that, when combined with a physical movement (like squeezing your fist), can signal the brain to *instantly* recall

experiences of success. When you use the cue word and perform the physical movement, you'll get passionate about what lies ahead. Go out, train, and perform!

6. *Consistent Resilient Action.* CRA is the difference between your dreams remaining a fantasy or becoming real. CRA is the internal drive that creates the enthusiasm that keeps you working harder toward your athletic goals. You won't give up when things don't go right the first time; you'll go back and do it again. If you can't go through the obstacle ahead, you'll go around it; if you can't go around it, you'll go over it; if you can't go over it, you'll go under it. With belief and all the emotion you can muster, you'll stretch yourself and find a way.

Make Your Dreams Real

At the 1992 Olympics in Barcelona, gymnast Trent Dimas won the gold medal on the horizontal bar, the first gold won by an American gymnast in a nonboycotted Olympics in thirty-six years. He made the most of his natural talents and thousands of hours of preparation, both in and out of the gymnasium. In the minutes before he competed at the Olympics, while waiting to give what he hoped would be the performance of his life, he closed his eyes, quieted his mind, blocked out the distractions around him, and began to visualize.

Dimas recalled, "I never watched the competitors and I didn't look at their scores." In fact, Dimas kept his eyes shut as one gymnast, then another, went through their routines. He stayed relaxed and created an internal peace that would serve him well, while focusing on his own routine and visualizing himself performing perfectly. "There was nothing I could do about the competition," he said. "But there was a lot I could do to keep my mind quiet and give my body the freedom to do what I knew it could do well." When it was finally his time to compete, he gave an absolutely flawless performance and was rewarded with scores of perfect 10's.

Never lose sight of your Desire Statement. Repeat it again and again. Begin each day with your goals in mind. Most people believe that to excel at their sport they have to spend more and more time on the training field. But once your overall training program becomes well rounded and you integrate the Mental Edge into it, you can dramatically transform the level at which you compete. As I described in chapter 1, you need about six hours to learn the tools in this book. After that it's just a matter of practicing them fifteen to twenty minutes a day. The Mental Edge will keep you mentally tough and maintain your belief that you can beat anyone, at any time, week in, week out.

Before we wrap up and send you out on your own to master the Mental Edge, let's do a final exercise together.

▪ ENJOYING YOUR SUCCESS ▪

To begin, sit in a comfortable chair, shut your eyes, and get in touch with what you want to accomplish athletically. Take a few moments to briefly see that accomplishment in your mind's eye. Don't worry about the details now. You'll fill them in at some point. But see your outcome. See your-self performing as you'd like to.

Now, perform a "tension blowout." Take a deep belly breath . . . hold it for five seconds . . . then blow it out, expelling all the air. . . . Then take a couple gentle, soothing, normal breaths. . . .

Inhale another deep belly breath, and as you do, make a fist with your non-dominant hand. . . . Hold your breath for three seconds, and then re-lease it, opening your fist slowly at the same time. Feel the sensations of relaxation envelop you. . . .

Next, see your Performance Cue (a word asso-ciated with relaxation) in the palm of your open hand, take another deep breath, exhale, and squeeze the thumb and forefinger of your hand to-gether, firmly but gently, for about one second. Feel your sense of relaxation intensify even fur-ther. . . .

While you enjoy this sensation allow yourself to see the end result of all your hard work on the athletic field. Notice how good these achievements make you feel. See the expression on your face, the posture of your body, and the sounds of congratu-lations from those around you. What are they say-ing to you? What are you saying to yourself?

Now, ponder some of the obstacles you over-came to reach your goals. . . . Reflect on how your skill levels have improved, and the small steps you took that turned into huge achievements. . . . Con-template the dedication it took to get to where you wanted to be. . . . How did you discipline your-self? . . . What are the obstacles you overcame? . . .

Enjoy the moment. And answer the question, "Was it all worth it?"

In this book, I've covered plenty of information that will help you perform better as an athlete, no matter what your current level. The Mental Edge exercises can become the cornerstones of your own excellence in sports. If you haven't already started using them, begin doing so now, taking advantage of what you've learned. Remember, good things *don't* come to those who wait; they come to those who go out and get them. For procrastinators there will only be a lot of disappointments, and regrets over never having taken full advantage of the opportunities available to them.

My wish for you is that you strengthen your tenacity to succeed, not only in sports, but in life. Develop a winning attitude—on the playing field, in school, and in the work world. As that happens, you'll soon become a person who's extremely happy with what you've accomplished in every aspect of your life.

I look forward to hearing about your improvements. Drop me a line at the address in the back of this book. Let me know how you're doing. Remember, you already have everything inside of you necessary to become as great as you desire. The Mental Edge will activate that sleeping giant within, and turn you into the athlete and the person you want to become.

Additional Reading

Cox, Richard H. *Sport Psychology: Concepts and Applications*. Dubuque, Ia.: W.C. Brown, 1985.

Jones, J. Graham, and Lew Hardy, eds. *Stress and Performance in Sport*. New York: Wiley, 1990.

Livingston, Michael K. *Mental Discipline: The Pursuit of Peak Performance*. Champaign, Ill.: Human Kinetics, 1989.

Martens, Rainer, Robin S. Vealey, and Damon Burton. *Competitive Anxiety in Sport*. Champaign, Ill.: Human Kinetics, 1990.

Morgan, Aidan P., ed. *The Psychology of Concentration in Sport Performers: A Cognitive Analysis*. Hove, England: Psychology Press, 1996.

Morgan, William P., ed. *Contemporary Readings in Sports Psychology*. Springfield, Ill.: Thomas, 1970.

Orlick, Terry. *In Pursuit of Excellence: How to Win in Sport and Life Through Mental Training*. Champaign, Ill.: Human Kinetics, 1990.

Singer, Robert N., Milledge Murphey, and L. Keith Tennant. *Handbook of Research on Sport Psychology*. New York: Macmillan, 1993.

Van Raalte, Judy L., and Britton W. Brewer, eds. *Exploring Sport and Exercise Psychology*. Washington, D.C.: American Psychological Association, 1996.

For more information about developing your Mental Edge, including the availability of consulting, seminars, and audiotapes and other materials, contact us at the address and phone number below. All Mental Edge exercises are available on audiotape. Sport-specific tapes are also available.

We also can provide you with information about the Performance Zone Nutrition Program designed for your unique metabolism and sport.

The Mental Edge
P.O. Box 1269
San Juan Capistrano, CA 92693

Phone: (800) 828-EDGE
           (949) 493-3193

For a free copy of the performance enhancing newsletter, *Sports to the Max—How to Eat, Think, and Train Like a Champion,* please complete and mail to the address on page 176.

Name _____

Address _____

City _____ State _____ Zip _____

Phone (optional) _____

What is your primary sport?

How long have you been playing?

What is your skill level? (circle one)

professional	world-class amateur	college
high school	grade school	competitive recreational
recreation		

Index